TECH WITH HEART

INTEGRATING ETHICS INTO DIGITAL LEARNING

DR. MINAKSHI BANSAL

Contents

Contents

Contents

Prayer

"Om Bhadram Karnebhih Shrinuyama Devah

Bhadram Pashyemakshabhiryajatrah

Sthirairangais Tushtuvamsastanubhih

Vyashema Devahitam Yadayuh

Svasti Na Indro Vriddhashravah

Svasti Nah Pusha Vishwavedah

Svasti Nastarkshyo Arishtanemih

Svasti No Brihaspatir Dadhatu

Om Shantih Shantih Shantih"

This mantra is a prayer for universal well-being, invoking the blessings of various deities for protection, health, and happiness. It emphasizes the importance of experiencing the auspicious through all senses and living a life aligned with divine purpose. The repetition of "Shantih" at the end signifies a deep desire for peace in the individual, the environment, and the universe at large. This mantra is often recited as a prayer for peace, prosperity, and the physical and spiritual well-being of all beings.

About The Author

This book represents the culmination of extensive research and meticulous analysis, incorporating a diverse range of sources, including numerous books, scholarly studies, and personal experiences. Additionally, I have scoured various websites to gather relevant information and data essential for the compilation of this work. I have taken every precaution to ensure the accuracy of the information presented and have diligently cited all sources to acknowledge their contributions.

From her earliest days, Minakshi was distinguished by an insatiable appetite for reading. Her literary universe was inhabited by characters and narratives that spanned ethical tales, motivational and inspirational stories, and the mythic parables imbued with life lessons. This voracious reading habit was not merely for personal edification but was driven by a desire to distill and disseminate the essence of these narratives to foster the development of students and peers alike. She was particularly captivated by the lives and teachings of historical figures and spiritual leaders such as Adi Shankaracharya, Swami Vivekananda, Dr. APJ Abdul Kalam, Mahamana Pandit Madan Mohan Malviya, Mahatma Gandhi, Sardar Vallabhai Patel, and Vinoba Bhave, among others. Their philosophies and life stories fueled her ambition to embody their ideals of resilience, selflessness, and relentless pursuit of knowledge.

Dr. Minakshi's academic and practical engagement with psychology has been equally noteworthy. As a research scholar, her focus has been on exploring the intricate tapestry of the human psyche, aiming to unlock the potential for psychological well-being and societal harmony. Her scholarly work is complemented by her active involvement in social work, where she employs her academic insights to make tangible differences in the lives of the underprivileged. Her endeavours in social work are characterized by an innovative approach that combines traditional wisdom with contemporary psychological practices to address the multifaceted challenges faced by these communities.

Her artistic talents, another facet of her diverse capabilities, are not merely a personal passion but also serve as a medium through which she communicates and connects with others. Her art, rich in symbolism and emotional depth, reflects her philosophical inquiries and social concerns, offering viewers a glimpse into the breadth of her intellect and the depth of her compassion.

In addition to her contributions to the arts and social sciences, Dr. Minakshi has embraced the healing arts of Pranic Healing, mastering the techniques developed by Master Choa Kok Sui. This practice, which focuses on the manipulation of Prana or life energy to heal the body and aura, has been both a personal journey of discovery and a means through which she extends her healing touch to others. Her proficiency in Pranic Healing is complemented by her advocacy and teaching of various forms of meditation aimed at rejuvenation, personal betterment, and the cultivation of harmony within individuals and communities alike.

Dr. Minakshi's life is a narrative of relentless pursuit, not just of personal achievement but of the upliftment and empowerment of society at large. Her diverse interests and talents—spanning the arts, literature, psychology, and the healing practices—converge on a singular path of service. She embodies the spirit of the luminaries who inspired her, channelling their legacy through her actions and teachings. Through her books, art, and social initiatives, she continues to inspire a new generation to embark on their own journeys of self-discovery, resilience, and altruism.

Her commitment to social betterment, particularly her focus on uplifting underprivileged children, reflects a deep understanding of the transformative potential of education and personal development. By integrating her knowledge of psychology, her artistic sensibilities, and her healing practices, Dr. Bansal has developed a holistic approach to social work that addresses both the immediate needs and the long-term well-being of the communities she serves.

As an author, Dr. Minakshi's writings offer a blend of inspirational insights, practical wisdom, and reflective contemplations drawn from her extensive reading and life experiences. Her books serve as a guide for those seeking to navigate the complexities of life with grace, resilience, and purpose. Through her narratives, she extends an invitation to her readers to explore the depths of their own potential and to contribute meaningfully to the collective well-being of society.

In Dr. Minakshi Bansal, we find a remarkable synthesis of the artist, the scholar, the healer, and the social activist. Her life's work stands as a beacon of hope and a source of inspiration for individuals seeking to make a difference in the world. Her story is a compelling reminder of the power of individual action, rooted in compassion and driven by a profound commitment to the betterment of humanity. Dr. Minakshi's legacy is not just in the tangible outcomes of her efforts but in the enduring spirit of inquiry, empathy, and service that she embodies.

ᐅᐅᐅ

Preface

The rapid pace of technological advancement has undeniably transformed every aspect of our lives, and education is no exception. As an educator deeply passionate about the potential of technology to enhance learning, I have witnessed firsthand the remarkable benefits it can bring. From virtual classrooms to interactive learning tools, the digital age offers unparalleled opportunities for engagement, collaboration, and access to knowledge. However, with these advancements come significant ethical challenges that cannot be overlooked. This book was born out of my commitment to addressing these challenges and my belief that ethical considerations must be at the forefront of digital learning.

My journey into the world of education began long before the ubiquity of digital tools. I remember the days of chalkboards and handwritten notes, when the physical presence of a teacher in a classroom was the cornerstone of learning. Over time, I embraced the digital revolution with enthusiasm, integrating technology into my teaching practices and witnessing its transformative power. Yet, as I delved deeper into the digital landscape, I became increasingly aware of the ethical dilemmas that accompanied these advancements. Issues such as data privacy, digital equity, intellectual property, and the psychological impact of constant connectivity began to surface, demanding thoughtful consideration and action.

This book is a culmination of my reflections, experiences, and research on the intersection of technology and ethics in education. It is a call to action for educators, students, policymakers, and all stakeholders in the educational ecosystem to prioritize ethics in the digital age. The aim is not to deter the use of technology in learning but to ensure that its implementation is guided by principles that uphold the dignity, rights, and well-being of all individuals involved.

One of the most pressing ethical concerns in digital learning is the issue of privacy. The collection and analysis of vast amounts of data have become integral to many educational technologies, offering valuable insights into student performance and engagement. However, this data collection often comes at the expense of student privacy. As educators, we have a duty to protect the personal information of our students and to be transparent about how their data is being used. This involves not only adhering to legal requirements but also fostering a culture of trust and respect. Students should feel confident that their privacy is safeguarded and that their data is used ethically and responsibly.

In addition to privacy, the digital divide presents a significant challenge to equitable education. Despite the widespread availability of digital tools, access to technology remains unevenly distributed. Students from underserved communities often face barriers to accessing the devices and internet connectivity necessary for digital learning. This disparity exacerbates existing inequalities and hinders the educational progress of many students. Addressing this issue requires a concerted effort to bridge the digital divide, ensuring that all students have the resources they need to succeed. This involves advocating for policies that provide technology access to underserved communities, designing inclusive learning materials, and supporting initiatives that promote digital literacy for all.

The ethical use of artificial intelligence (AI) and machine learning in education is another critical area of concern. While these technologies offer promising opportunities for personalized learning, they also raise significant ethical questions. AI algorithms can perpetuate biases and inequalities if not carefully designed and monitored. As educators, it is our responsibility to ensure that AI tools are used ethically and that their potential biases are addressed.

This involves advocating for transparency in the development and deployment of AI technologies, educating ourselves and our students about the ethical implications of AI, and promoting critical thinking about the technology we use. By approaching AI with an ethical mindset, we can harness its potential while minimizing its risks.

Digital citizenship is a fundamental aspect of ethical digital learning. In an age where online interactions are a daily reality, teaching students to be responsible digital citizens is crucial. This involves promoting empathy and respect in online interactions, educating students about the potential consequences of cyberbullying, and encouraging the thoughtful and respectful sharing of opinions and information. As educators, we have a unique opportunity to shape the digital behavior of our students, fostering a culture of kindness, respect, and integrity in the digital world.

The creation and consumption of digital content also carry significant ethical implications. In an era where anyone can publish content online, the lines between credible information and misinformation can become blurred. Educators must guide students in understanding their ethical responsibilities as content creators and consumers. This includes teaching them the importance of accuracy, the impact of misinformation, and the need for respectful and constructive communication. Additionally, students should be taught to critically evaluate the information they encounter online, discerning credible sources from unreliable ones. By promoting ethical content creation and consumption, we can help students become more discerning and responsible digital citizens.

The mental and emotional well-being of students is another critical consideration in ethical digital learning. The digital world, with its constant connectivity, can be overwhelming and lead to issues such as screen fatigue, anxiety, and social isolation. As educators, we must be mindful of these challenges and take steps to support the well-being of our students. This includes promoting healthy digital habits, such as taking regular breaks from screens, encouraging face-to-face interactions, and fostering a balanced approach to technology use. We should also create a supportive environment where students feel comfortable discussing their digital experiences and any associated challenges. By prioritizing well-being, we can help students navigate the digital world in a healthy and balanced manner.

Ethical digital learning also involves the responsible use of digital tools and resources. As educators, we must be discerning in our selection of digital tools, ensuring that they align with ethical standards and support educational goals. This includes evaluating the data privacy policies of digital tools, considering the potential for bias, and ensuring that the tools are accessible and inclusive. By carefully selecting and using digital tools, we can model ethical behavior and provide students with a positive digital learning experience.

Our role as educators extends beyond the classroom. We must also advocate for ethical policies at the institutional and governmental levels. This involves staying informed about the latest developments in educational technology and being proactive in addressing emerging ethical issues. We can contribute to policy discussions, best practices, and collaborate with other stakeholders to promote ethical standards in digital learning. By taking an active role in shaping the ethical landscape of digital education, we can help ensure that the benefits of technology are realized while minimizing its risks.

Learners, too, have a vital role in championing ethics in digital learning. They must be proactive in understanding and upholding ethical standards, taking responsibility for their actions in the digital world. This includes being honest in their academic work, respecting the privacy and rights of others, and engaging in respectful and constructive online behavior. Learners should also be critical thinkers, questioning the information they encounter and making informed decisions about the digital tools and resources they use. By taking an active role in promoting ethical digital learning, learners can contribute to a positive and respectful digital learning environment.

Collaboration between educators and learners is essential for fostering an ethical digital learning environment. By working together, we can create a culture of mutual respect, integrity, and responsibility. This involves open communication, where educators and learners can discuss ethical issues, their experiences, and learn from each other. Collaborative projects that focus on ethical digital practices can also be an effective way to reinforce these values. By fostering a collaborative approach, we can build a strong foundation for ethical digital learning.

The integration of ethics into digital learning is not a one-time effort but an ongoing process. As technology continues to evolve, new ethical challenges will emerge, requiring continuous reflection and adaptation. Educators and learners must remain vigilant, continually assessing and updating their ethical practices to address new developments. This involves staying informed about technological advancements, participating in ongoing professional development, and being open to new ideas and approaches. By committing to ongoing ethical reflection and adaptation, we can ensure that digital learning remains a positive and enriching experience.

This book is a call to action, a reminder that the integration of ethics into digital learning is a d responsibility. As an educator, I am committed to this cause, and I invite you to join me in this journey. Together, we can create a digital learning environment that is both enriching and ethical, one that respects the dignity and rights of all individuals involved. Let us embrace the potential of technology while upholding the principles of integrity, privacy, inclusivity, and well-being. By doing so, we can harness the power of technology to create a better and more equitable educational future.

● XX ●

Dr. Minakshi Bansal
Social Activist
Ahmedabad, Gujarat, Bharat

ԵԵԵ

ONE

THE WHY BEHIND ETHICS: EXPLORING THE CRUCIAL ROLE OF ETHICS IN THE DIGITAL AGE AND ITS IMPACT ON LEARNING.

In an era defined by rapid technological advancements and the ubiquity of digital platforms, the question of ethics has taken on a new urgency. While the digital age has ushered in unprecedented opportunities for learning and connection, it has also brought forth a myriad of ethical challenges that cannot be ignored. The imperative to integrate ethics into digital learning is not merely a matter of academic discourse; it is a critical endeavor that shapes the way we interact with technology, information, and each other in the virtual realm.

At its core, ethics is a system of moral principles that guide our behavior and decision-making. In the digital age, these principles are put to the test in novel and complex ways. The ease with which information can be accessed, shared, and manipulated online has created an environment ripe for ethical dilemmas. From issues of privacy and data security to the spread of misinformation and online harassment, the ethical implications of digital interactions are far-reaching and profound.

The importance of ethics in digital learning becomes evident when we consider the formative nature of education. Learning is not solely about acquiring knowledge and skills; it is also about developing values, character, and a sense of social responsibility. When students engage with digital tools and platforms, they are not simply passive recipients of information; they are active participants in a virtual community where their actions have consequences. By integrating ethics into digital learning, we equip students with the critical thinking skills and ethical frameworks necessary to navigate this complex landscape responsibly.

One of the most pressing ethical concerns in the digital age is the erosion of privacy. The vast amount of personal data collected and shared online raises questions about who owns this data, how it is used, and what safeguards are in place to protect it. Students need to understand the potential risks associated with sharing their information online and the importance of safeguarding their digital footprints. By incorporating discussions about privacy into digital learning, we empower students to make informed choices about their online presence and to advocate for stronger privacy protections.

Another critical ethical issue in digital learning is the proliferation of misinformation and "fake news." The internet has become a breeding ground for false or misleading information, which can easily spread and influence public opinion. This phenomenon poses a serious threat to the integrity of information and the ability of students to discern fact from fiction. To combat this, educators need to teach students how to evaluate the credibility of online sources, identify bias, and think critically about the information they encounter. By doing so, we cultivate a generation of informed and discerning digital citizens who can actively participate in democratic discourse.

The digital divide, which refers to the unequal access to technology and the internet, is another ethical challenge that must be addressed in digital learning. While some students have access to high-speed internet and the latest devices, others are left behind due to socioeconomic factors or geographical limitations. This disparity can exacerbate existing educational inequalities and hinder the learning opportunities of disadvantaged students. To bridge this divide, educators and policymakers need to work together to ensure that all students have access to the tools and resources necessary for digital learning. This includes providing affordable internet access, loaning devices to students in need, and creating offline learning materials for those without reliable connectivity.

Beyond these specific issues, there is a broader ethical imperative to cultivate a digital learning environment that is inclusive, respectful, and supportive. Online interactions can easily devolve into incivility and harassment, particularly when anonymity is involved. It is crucial to establish clear guidelines for online behavior and to foster a culture of respect and empathy in virtual classrooms. This involves teaching students how to communicate effectively online, resolve conflicts peacefully, and appreciate diversity of perspectives.

The integration of ethics into digital learning is not simply an add-on or an afterthought; it is a fundamental aspect of preparing students for the challenges and opportunities of the 21st century. By equipping students with the ethical knowledge, skills, and dispositions necessary to navigate the digital world responsibly, we empower them to become active and engaged citizens who can make positive contributions to their communities and the world at large.

ᑭᑭᑭ

"In the digital age, integrity is our most valuable asset. Uphold it, teach it, and live by it. The future of education depends on it."

TWO

DIGITAL NATIVES, ETHICAL DILEMMAS: UNDERSTANDING THE CHALLENGES FACED BY TODAY'S LEARNERS IN NAVIGATING ETHICAL CHOICES ONLINE.

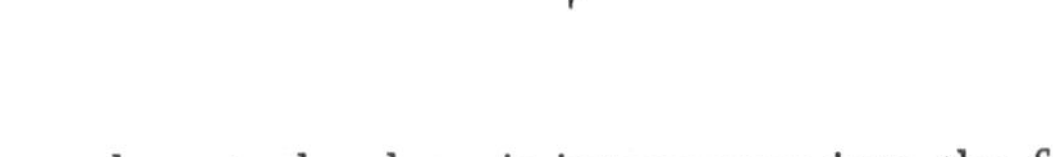

In an age where technology is interwoven into the fabric of daily life, today's learners, often referred to as "digital natives," have grown up immersed in the digital world. They are fluent in the language of social media, online gaming, and instant messaging.

While this digital fluency brings a wealth of opportunities, it also presents a unique set of ethical challenges. As these learners navigate the vast and often uncharted territory of the internet, they are confronted with a barrage of ethical dilemmas that can be difficult to decipher.

One of the most pressing ethical dilemmas faced by digital natives is the issue of online identity and reputation. In the virtual world, individuals have the ability to curate and present themselves in ways that may not fully reflect their offline persona. This can lead to issues of authenticity, misrepresentation, and even deception. For young learners, who are still in the process of forming their identities, the pressure to conform to online norms and expectations can be overwhelming. The pursuit of online validation through likes, s, and followers can distort their sense of self-worth and lead to harmful behaviors. Educators and parents have a crucial role to play in helping digital natives understand the importance of authenticity, honesty, and integrity in their online interactions.

Another significant ethical challenge for digital natives is the pervasive nature of cyberbullying and online harassment. The anonymity and lack of physical proximity afforded by the internet can embolden individuals to engage in hurtful and abusive behavior that they might not exhibit in face-to-face interactions. This can have devastating consequences for the victims, leading to emotional distress, social isolation, and even suicidal ideation. It is imperative that digital natives are educated about the potential harm caused by cyberbullying and the importance of treating others with respect and empathy online. Schools and communities need to create safe spaces where victims of cyberbullying can seek help and support without fear of judgment or retribution.

The issue of intellectual property and plagiarism is also a major ethical concern for digital natives. The vast amount of information readily available online can blur the lines between original work and copied content. For students who are accustomed to cutting and pasting information from various sources, the concept of plagiarism may not always be clear. This can lead to unintentional academic dishonesty and a lack of understanding of the importance of giving credit to the original creators of content. Educators need to explicitly teach students about copyright laws, fair use, and the ethical implications of plagiarism. They also need to provide guidance on how to properly cite sources and create original work in a digital environment.

The digital divide also presents a significant ethical dilemma for digital natives. While some learners have access to high-speed internet, the latest devices, and a wealth of educational resources, others are left behind due to socioeconomic factors or geographical limitations. This unequal access to technology can exacerbate existing educational inequalities and create a "digital underclass." It is important to acknowledge this disparity and work towards creating more equitable access to digital learning opportunities. This may involve providing subsidized internet access, loaning devices to students in need, and creating offline learning materials for those without reliable connectivity.

Furthermore, the increasing reliance on artificial intelligence (AI) and algorithms in digital learning raises ethical questions about the role of technology in education. While AI can personalize learning experiences and provide tailored feedback, there are concerns about bias, transparency, and the potential for algorithms to perpetuate existing inequalities. It is important to critically examine the ethical implications of AI in education and ensure that it is used in ways that are fair, transparent, and beneficial to all learners.

In addition to these specific challenges, there is a broader ethical imperative to cultivate a digital learning environment that is inclusive, respectful, and supportive. The internet can be a platform for both positive and negative interactions. It is crucial to foster a culture of digital citizenship where learners understand their rights and responsibilities online. This involves teaching them how to communicate effectively, resolve conflicts peacefully, and appreciate diversity of perspectives. It also means educating them about the potential consequences of their online actions and the importance of being mindful of their digital footprint.

In conclusion, digital natives face a multitude of ethical dilemmas as they navigate the complex landscape of the internet. These challenges range from issues of online identity and cyberbullying to concerns about intellectual property, the digital divide, and the role of AI in education. By addressing these dilemmas head-on and integrating ethics into digital learning, we can empower digital natives to become responsible, ethical, and engaged citizens of the digital world. Educators, parents, and policymakers all have a role to play in this endeavor. By fostering a culture of digital citizenship and providing guidance and support, we can help digital natives navigate the ethical challenges of the digital age and harness the power of technology for good.

ᗘᗘᗘ

"Privacy in education is not a luxury; it is a
fundamental right. As we embrace technology, we
must also protect our students' personal
information. Transparency and respect are key."

THREE

Beyond the Click: Unpacking the Ethics Behind Online Behavior, from Social Media to Information Sharing.

In the digital age, the seemingly simple act of clicking a mouse or tapping a screen can have far-reaching consequences. Our online behavior, whether on social media platforms, forums, or through the sharing of information, has ethical implications that extend beyond the virtual realm. The interconnectedness of the internet means that our actions can ripple out and affect others in ways we may not anticipate. Understanding the ethics behind online behavior is essential for navigating the digital landscape responsibly and fostering a more ethical online environment.

One of the most pressing ethical issues in online behavior is the spread of misinformation and "fake news." The ease with which false or misleading information can be disseminated online poses a significant threat to the integrity of information and public discourse. Misinformation can have real-world consequences, from influencing elections to fueling social unrest. It is crucial to critically evaluate the sources of information we encounter online, verify claims before sharing them, and be mindful of the potential harm caused by spreading false narratives.

The power of social media to shape public opinion and influence behavior is undeniable. However, this power can be wielded for both good and ill. The ethics of social media usage involve considering the impact of our posts, comments, and s on others. Engaging in online harassment, hate speech, or the spread of harmful stereotypes can have devastating consequences for individuals and communities. It is important to promote respectful and inclusive dialogue online, avoid engaging in or amplifying harmful content, and use our platforms to uplift and empower others.

Privacy is another critical ethical concern in online behavior. The vast amount of personal data collected by companies and governments raises questions about who owns this data, how it is used, and what safeguards are in place to protect it. The potential for misuse of personal information, such as identity theft or discrimination, underscores the importance of safeguarding our privacy online. This involves being mindful of the information we , adjusting privacy settings on social media platforms, and advocating for stronger data protection laws.

The ethics of online behavior also extend to our interactions with others in virtual spaces. Cyberbullying, online harassment, and other forms of digital aggression can have serious psychological and emotional consequences for victims. It is important to treat others with respect and empathy online, avoid engaging in or condoning harmful behavior, and report instances of abuse to the appropriate authorities. Creating a safe and inclusive online environment requires collective effort and a commitment to upholding ethical standards of conduct.

The issue of intellectual property also plays a significant role in the ethics of online behavior. The ease with which digital content can be copied and d raises questions about ownership, copyright, and fair use. Sharing copyrighted material without permission can harm creators and undermine their livelihoods. It is important to respect intellectual property rights, give credit to original creators, and use content ethically and responsibly.

The anonymity afforded by the internet can be both a blessing and a curse. While it can empower individuals to express themselves freely and challenge authority, it can also embolden them to engage in harmful behavior without fear of consequences. The ethics of anonymity involve balancing the right to free expression with the responsibility to avoid causing harm to others. It is important to use anonymity ethically, avoiding the temptation to engage in online harassment, trolling, or other forms of digital aggression.

The concept of digital citizenship encompasses the rights and responsibilities of individuals in the online world. It involves understanding the ethical implications of online behavior, promoting digital literacy and critical thinking, and advocating for a more just and equitable digital environment. Digital citizenship education is essential for empowering individuals to navigate the digital landscape responsibly and make informed decisions about their online actions.

The ethics of online behavior are not static; they evolve alongside technology and social norms. As new digital platforms and technologies emerge, new ethical challenges arise. It is important to stay informed about these emerging challenges and adapt our ethical frameworks accordingly. This involves engaging in ongoing discussions about the ethical implications of technology, promoting digital literacy, and advocating for policies that protect individual rights and promote social good in the digital age.

In conclusion, the ethics of online behavior encompass a wide range of issues, from the spread of misinformation and privacy concerns to cyberbullying and intellectual property rights. Understanding these ethical challenges is crucial for navigating the digital landscape responsibly and fostering a more ethical online environment. By promoting digital citizenship, critical thinking, and ethical decision-making, we can create a digital world that is more equitable, inclusive, and respectful of individual rights and dignity.

ϷϷϷ

"Inclusivity in digital learning is essential for equitable education. Every student deserves access to the tools and resources needed for success. Bridging the digital divide must be our priority."

❧❧❧

FOUR

The Algorithm's Shadow: Examining the Ethical Implications of AI and Algorithms in Educational Technology.

In the digital age, the rise of artificial intelligence (AI) and algorithms has revolutionized various sectors, including education. Educational technology, powered by AI and algorithms, offers numerous benefits such as personalized learning, adaptive assessments, and intelligent tutoring systems. However, the integration of AI and algorithms in educational technology also raises significant ethical implications that warrant careful examination.

One of the primary concerns is the potential for algorithmic bias. Algorithms are not inherently neutral; they are designed and trained by humans, who may inadvertently introduce their biases into the system. In educational technology, algorithmic bias can manifest in various ways, such as favoring certain demographics over others, perpetuating stereotypes, or limiting access to certain opportunities. For instance, a biased algorithm might recommend different learning paths for students based on their gender or socioeconomic background, leading to unequal outcomes. It is crucial to ensure that algorithms used in educational technology are transparent, fair, and free from discriminatory biases.

Another ethical consideration is the issue of data privacy and security. Educational technology platforms often collect vast amounts of student data, including personal information, academic records, and behavioral patterns. This data can be used to personalize learning experiences, but it also raises concerns about who has access to this data, how it is used, and whether it is adequately protected from unauthorized access or misuse. The potential for data breaches and the misuse of student data for commercial purposes necessitate robust privacy policies and stringent security measures to safeguard the sensitive information of learners.

The increasing reliance on AI and algorithms in educational decision-making raises questions about accountability and transparency. When algorithms are used to determine student placements, grades, or access to resources, it is important to understand how these decisions are made and who is responsible for them. The lack of transparency in algorithmic decision-making can lead to a lack of trust and raise concerns about fairness and equity. It is crucial to ensure that algorithmic decisions are explainable and that there are mechanisms in place for recourse and appeal in case of errors or biases.

The use of AI in educational technology also raises concerns about the potential impact on the role of teachers. While AI can automate certain tasks and provide valuable insights, it is important to recognize that teachers play a crucial role in the educational process. They provide emotional support, mentorship, and guidance that cannot be replicated by machines. The integration of AI should complement and enhance the role of teachers, not replace them. It is important to ensure that teachers are equipped with the necessary skills to utilize AI effectively and that they retain their autonomy and agency in the classroom.

The potential for AI and algorithms to create filter bubbles and echo chambers is another ethical concern. When algorithms personalize content based on individual preferences and past behavior, they can inadvertently limit exposure to diverse perspectives and reinforce existing beliefs. This can hinder critical thinking and lead to a narrowing of worldview. It is important to ensure that educational technology platforms expose learners to a wide range of viewpoints and encourage them to engage with diverse ideas.

The use of AI in assessment and evaluation also raises ethical questions. While AI can provide more efficient and objective assessments, there are concerns about the validity and reliability of AI-generated scores. It is important to ensure that AI-based assessments are aligned with learning objectives, free from bias, and provide meaningful feedback to learners. The use of AI in high-stakes assessments, such as standardized tests, warrants careful consideration and ongoing evaluation to ensure fairness and equity.

The ethical implications of AI and algorithms in educational technology are complex and multifaceted. It is important to engage in ongoing dialogue and debate about these issues, involving educators, researchers, policymakers, and learners themselves. Ethical guidelines and regulations are necessary to ensure that AI is used responsibly and ethically in educational settings. This includes ensuring transparency, fairness, accountability, and the protection of privacy.

Furthermore, it is crucial to prioritize human values and ethical considerations in the development and deployment of educational technology. This means designing algorithms that are transparent, explainable, and free from bias. It also means ensuring that AI is used to enhance, not replace, the role of teachers and that it promotes equity and inclusivity in education. By addressing the ethical implications of AI and algorithms, we can harness the power of technology to create a more just, equitable, and empowering educational landscape for all learners.

ӬӬӬ

"Artificial intelligence holds great promise for personalized learning, but it must be used ethically. Vigilance against bias and transparency in algorithms are crucial. Educators must lead the way in responsible AI use."

FIVE

PRIVACY IN THE PIXELATED WORLD: PROTECTING PERSONAL INFORMATION AND TEACHING DIGITAL PRIVACY SKILLS TO LEARNERS.

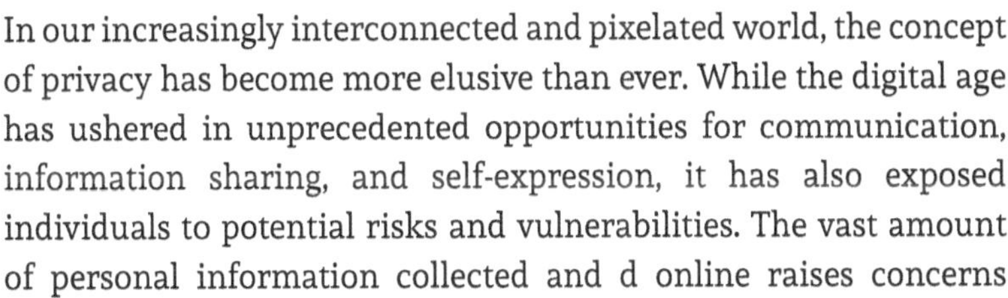

In our increasingly interconnected and pixelated world, the concept of privacy has become more elusive than ever. While the digital age has ushered in unprecedented opportunities for communication, information sharing, and self-expression, it has also exposed individuals to potential risks and vulnerabilities. The vast amount of personal information collected and d online raises concerns about who has access to this data, how it is used, and what safeguards are in place to protect it. Protecting personal information and teaching digital privacy skills to learners has become a paramount concern in today's digital landscape.

The digital footprint we leave behind through our online activities can have far-reaching consequences. From social media posts and online purchases to browsing history and location data, our personal information is constantly being collected, analyzed, and potentially exploited. Data breaches, identity theft, and online harassment are just a few of the risks associated with the unchecked flow of personal information in the digital realm. It is crucial to understand the value of our personal data and take proactive steps to protect it from unauthorized access or misuse.

One of the fundamental principles of privacy protection is informed consent. Individuals should have the right to know what data is being collected about them, how it will be used, and who will have access to it. This information should be presented in a clear and understandable manner, allowing individuals to make informed decisions about whether to their data. It is important to read privacy policies carefully, be wary of vague or overly broad terms, and exercise caution when sharing personal information online.

Another crucial aspect of privacy protection is data minimization. Organizations should collect only the minimum amount of personal data necessary to achieve their legitimate purposes. This means avoiding the collection of unnecessary or irrelevant data and implementing measures to securely dispose of data that is no longer needed. By minimizing the amount of personal data collected, we reduce the potential for it to be compromised or misused.

Strong security measures are essential for safeguarding personal information from unauthorized access. This includes using strong passwords, enabling two-factor authentication, and keeping software up to date. It is also important to be vigilant about phishing scams, which are fraudulent attempts to obtain personal information through deceptive emails or websites. By staying informed about the latest security threats and best practices, we can reduce the risk of falling victim to cyberattacks.

Teaching digital privacy skills to learners is essential for empowering them to navigate the digital world safely and responsibly. This includes educating them about the potential risks associated with sharing personal information online, the importance of using strong passwords and privacy settings, and how to identify and avoid phishing scams. It also involves teaching them how to critically evaluate online sources of information, understand the terms and conditions of online services, and advocate for their privacy rights.

Parental guidance and supervision play a crucial role in protecting the privacy of young learners. Parents should be actively involved in their children's online activities, discuss the importance of privacy, and set clear boundaries for online behavior. They should also educate themselves about the privacy settings of online platforms and apps used by their children and ensure that these settings are appropriately configured to protect their children's personal information.

Schools also have a responsibility to teach digital privacy skills to students. This can be done through dedicated lessons, integration into existing curricula, or extracurricular activities. By providing students with the knowledge and skills to protect their privacy online, schools can empower them to become responsible digital citizens who can make informed decisions about their online behavior and advocate for their privacy rights.

In conclusion, protecting personal information and teaching digital privacy skills to learners is a critical imperative in the pixelated

world we live in. The vast amount of personal data collected and
d online raises concerns about privacy, security, and the potential
for misuse. By understanding the value of our personal data, being
mindful of the information we , and taking proactive steps to
protect our privacy, we can mitigate the risks associated with the
digital age. Educating learners about digital privacy empowers them
to navigate the online world safely and responsibly, making
informed decisions about their online behavior and advocating for
their privacy rights. By working together to prioritize privacy, we
can create a more secure and empowering digital environment for
all.

ppp

"Digital citizenship is more than just responsible use of technology. It is about empathy, respect, and understanding our role in the digital world. Educators have a duty to instill these values in their students."

SIX

CYBERBULLYING: THE SILENT THREAT: RECOGNIZING THE SIGNS OF CYBERBULLYING AND CREATING A SAFE ONLINE LEARNING ENVIRONMENT.

In the digital age, cyberbullying has emerged as a pervasive and insidious threat, casting a shadow over the online experiences of countless individuals, particularly young learners. Unlike traditional bullying, which often occurs in physical spaces, cyberbullying takes place in the virtual realm, where anonymity and the absence of physical boundaries can amplify its impact. Recognizing the signs of cyberbullying and creating a safe online learning environment is crucial for protecting the well-being and mental health of those targeted by this silent threat.

Cyberbullying manifests in various forms, including online harassment, denigration, impersonation, exclusion, and the spreading of rumors or lies. It can occur through various channels, such as social media platforms, messaging apps, online forums, and gaming communities. The anonymity afforded by the internet can embolden perpetrators to engage in harmful behavior that they might not exhibit in face-to-face interactions. The persistent and pervasive nature of cyberbullying can have devastating consequences for victims, leading to emotional distress, anxiety, depression, social isolation, and even suicidal ideation.

One of the challenges in addressing cyberbullying is its often subtle and insidious nature. Unlike physical bullying, which often leaves visible marks, cyberbullying can be harder to detect. Victims may suffer in silence, afraid to speak out or unsure of where to turn for help. It is crucial to be vigilant and recognize the signs of cyberbullying, which can include changes in mood or behavior, withdrawal from social activities, loss of interest in previously enjoyed activities, difficulty sleeping or concentrating, and unexplained physical ailments.

Creating a safe online learning environment requires a multi-faceted approach that involves educators, parents, students, and the wider community. Schools and educational institutions play a crucial role in preventing and addressing cyberbullying. This involves implementing comprehensive policies that clearly define cyberbullying, outline procedures for reporting and responding to incidents, and establish consequences for perpetrators. Educators should receive training on how to identify and address cyberbullying, as well as how to create a supportive and inclusive online learning environment.

Parents also have a crucial role to play in protecting their children from cyberbullying. This involves open communication with their children about their online activities, setting clear expectations for online behavior, and monitoring their children's use of technology. It is important for parents to be aware of the signs of cyberbullying and to create a safe space where their children feel comfortable discussing any concerns they may have. If a child is being cyberbullied, parents should take immediate action by documenting the incidents, reporting them to the relevant authorities, and seeking professional help if necessary.

Students themselves can also contribute to creating a safe online learning environment by being mindful of their own online behavior and standing up against cyberbullying when they witness it. This involves treating others with respect and empathy online, avoiding engaging in or condoning harmful behavior, and reporting instances of cyberbullying to trusted adults. By fostering a culture of kindness and respect online, students can create a more positive and inclusive digital community.

Technology companies also have a responsibility to address cyberbullying on their platforms. This involves implementing robust reporting mechanisms, providing resources for victims, and taking action against perpetrators. Social media platforms, in particular, should invest in developing tools and algorithms to detect and prevent cyberbullying, as well as educating users about the potential harm caused by this behavior.

The fight against cyberbullying requires a collective effort from all stakeholders. By working together to raise awareness, educate the public, and implement effective prevention and intervention strategies, we can create a safer and more inclusive online environment for all. This includes supporting research on cyberbullying, advocating for stronger laws and policies to protect victims, and investing in programs that promote digital literacy and responsible online behavior.

In conclusion, cyberbullying is a silent threat that can have devastating consequences for victims. Recognizing the signs of cyberbullying and creating a safe online learning environment is crucial for protecting the well-being and mental health of those targeted by this harmful behavior. By working together, we can create a digital world that is free from harassment, hate, and discrimination, where everyone feels safe, respected, and valued.

❦❦❦

"Creating and consuming digital content comes with ethical responsibilities. Accuracy, respect, and critical evaluation are paramount. Let us guide our students to be thoughtful digital citizens."

SEVEN

INTELLECTUAL PROPERTY 101. DEMYSTIFYING COPYRIGHT, PLAGIARISM, AND FAIR USE IN THE DIGITAL AGE.

In the digital age, the landscape of intellectual property has undergone a profound transformation. The ease with which information can be accessed, copied, and d online has blurred the lines between original creation and unauthorized reproduction. Understanding the concepts of copyright, plagiarism, and fair use has become more crucial than ever for navigating the ethical and legal complexities of the digital world.

At its core, intellectual property refers to creations of the mind, such as inventions, literary and artistic works, designs, and symbols. Copyright is a legal right that grants creators exclusive control over their original works, including the right to reproduce, distribute, display, and perform their creations. In the digital age, copyright protection extends to various forms of media, such as text, images, music, videos, and software. Copyright law aims to incentivize creativity and innovation by ensuring that creators can reap the rewards of their labor and invest in further creative endeavors.

Plagiarism, on the other hand, is the act of using someone else's work or ideas without proper attribution. It is a form of intellectual dishonesty that can have serious consequences, both academically and professionally. In the digital age, plagiarism has become more prevalent due to the ease with which information can be copied and pasted from online sources. However, the ethical and legal principles surrounding plagiarism remain unchanged. Whether it is copying and pasting text from a website without citation or using someone else's image without permission, plagiarism is a violation of copyright law and an act of academic misconduct.

Fair use is a legal doctrine that allows for the limited use of copyrighted material without permission from the copyright holder for purposes such as criticism, commentary, news reporting, teaching, scholarship, or research. Fair use is a complex and often misunderstood concept, with no clear-cut rules or guidelines. The determination of whether a particular use constitutes fair use depends on several factors, including the purpose and character of the use, the nature of the copyrighted work, the amount and substantiality of the portion used, and the effect of the use on the potential market for or value of the copyrighted work.

In the digital age, the concept of fair use has become increasingly relevant, as the internet has made it easier than ever to access and copyrighted material. However, the boundaries of fair use remain contested, and there is ongoing debate about how to apply this doctrine to new technologies and digital content. It is crucial to understand the principles of fair use and to exercise caution when using copyrighted material online.

The digital age has also brought about new challenges for enforcing copyright protection. The ease with which digital content can be copied and distributed online has made it more difficult for copyright holders to protect their works from unauthorized use. Digital Rights Management (DRM) technologies, which aim to restrict the use of digital content, have been implemented to combat copyright infringement. However, these technologies have also raised concerns about user rights and access to information.

Educating individuals about intellectual property, copyright, plagiarism, and fair use is crucial for fostering a culture of respect for creators' rights and responsible use of digital content. This includes teaching students how to properly cite sources, use Creative Commons licenses, and create original work. It also involves raising awareness about the ethical implications of plagiarism and the importance of supporting creators by purchasing or licensing their work.

Libraries and educational institutions play a crucial role in promoting understanding of intellectual property issues. They can offer workshops, tutorials, and resources on copyright, plagiarism, and fair use, as well as provide guidance on how to access and use copyrighted material responsibly. By fostering a culture of respect for intellectual property, we can ensure that creators are fairly compensated for their work and that the public has access to a rich and diverse array of creative content.

In conclusion, navigating the complex landscape of intellectual property in the digital age requires a nuanced understanding of copyright, plagiarism, and fair use. By respecting creators' rights, using content responsibly, and educating ourselves and others about these important issues, we can create a more ethical and sustainable digital ecosystem that supports creativity, innovation, and the free exchange of ideas.

❧❧❧

"The well-being of our students is as important as their academic success. In a world of constant connectivity, promoting healthy digital habits is crucial. Balance and support are key to navigating the digital landscape."

EIGHT

DIGITAL DIVIDE AND EQUITY: ADDRESSING THE ETHICAL IMPLICATIONS OF UNEQUAL ACCESS TO TECHNOLOGY AND EDUCATION.

In our increasingly digital world, the concept of the digital divide looms large. This divide refers to the gap between individuals, households, and communities who have access to digital technologies and those who do not. This gap has significant ethical implications for education and equity, as it can exacerbate existing social and economic inequalities, creating a "digital underclass" of individuals who are left behind in the digital age.

The digital divide manifests in various forms. It can be a matter of access to the internet, with some individuals having high-speed broadband connections while others have limited or no access. It can also be a matter of access to devices such as computers, tablets, and smartphones, with some individuals owning the latest technology while others lack even basic devices. Moreover, the digital divide is not just about access to hardware and connectivity; it is also about digital literacy, the skills and knowledge necessary to effectively use digital technologies.

The ethical implications of the digital divide are far-reaching. In education, it can create significant disparities in learning opportunities and outcomes. Students who have access to digital resources and tools are able to engage in online learning, access educational materials, and collaborate with peers from around the world. They are also better prepared for the digital workforce, where technological skills are increasingly in demand.

On the other hand, students without access to these resources are at a significant disadvantage. They may struggle to keep up with their peers, miss out on enriching educational experiences, and be less prepared for the digital economy.

The digital divide can also perpetuate existing social and economic inequalities. Those who are already marginalized, such as low-income families, racial and ethnic minorities, and individuals with disabilities, are disproportionately affected by the digital divide.

This can lead to a cycle of disadvantage, where lack of access to digital technologies further limits opportunities for education, employment, and civic participation.

Addressing the digital divide and its ethical implications requires a multi-pronged approach. One crucial step is to invest in infrastructure to ensure that all individuals have access to affordable and reliable broadband internet. This may involve government subsidies, public-private partnerships, or community-based initiatives to expand internet access in underserved areas.

Additionally, efforts should be made to provide affordable devices and digital literacy training to individuals who lack these resources.

Schools and libraries play a critical role in bridging the digital divide. They can provide access to computers and the internet, offer digital literacy workshops, and create inclusive learning environments where all students can thrive regardless of their technological background.

Educators also need to be trained on how to effectively integrate technology into their teaching practices and how to support students who may lack digital skills.

Beyond access and infrastructure, it is important to address the underlying social and economic factors that contribute to the digital divide. This includes addressing issues such as poverty, inequality, and discrimination. By creating a more equitable society, we can help to ensure that all individuals have the opportunity to participate fully in the digital age.

The private sector also has a role to play in addressing the digital divide. Technology companies can partner with schools, libraries, and community organizations to provide access to technology and digital literacy training. They can also develop affordable devices and software that are accessible to low-income individuals and families.

The digital divide is a complex issue with no easy solutions. However, it is an ethical imperative to address this divide and ensure that all individuals have equal opportunities to access and benefit from digital technologies.

By investing in infrastructure, providing access to devices and training, and addressing the underlying social and economic factors that contribute to the divide, we can create a more equitable and inclusive digital future for all.

♥♥♥

"The selection of digital tools must be guided by ethical standards. Privacy, accessibility, and inclusivity should be at the forefront. Educators must model responsible use to provide positive learning experiences."

❧❧❧

NINE

DESIGNING FOR ETHICS: CREATING EDUCATIONAL TECHNOLOGY TOOLS THAT PRIORITIZE ETHICAL CONSIDERATIONS.

In the rapidly evolving landscape of educational technology, ethical considerations have become paramount. Designing educational technology tools with ethics at the forefront is not just a moral imperative; it is essential for fostering a positive and equitable learning environment that benefits all students. By prioritizing ethical principles in the design process, we can create tools that empower learners, respect their privacy, promote fairness, and address potential biases.

The foundation of ethical design in educational technology lies in user-centeredness. This means putting the needs and interests of learners at the heart of the design process. Tools should be intuitive, accessible, and inclusive, catering to learners of diverse backgrounds and abilities. This involves considering factors suchas language, cultural context, learning styles, and accessibility needs. By designing tools that are user-friendly and adaptable, we can ensure that all learners have equal opportunities to benefit from educational technology.

Transparency is another crucial aspect of ethical design. Learners and educators should have a clear understanding of how educational technology tools work, what data they collect, and how that data is used. This involves providing clear and concise information about the algorithms, data collection practices, and privacy policies associated with the tool. Transparency builds trust and empowers users to make informed decisions about their participation in digital learning environments.

Privacy is a fundamental human right that should be protected in the design of educational technology. Tools should collect only the minimum amount of data necessary to achieve their educational purposes. This data should be securely stored and used only for legitimate educational purposes. Learners should have control over their personal information, including the ability to access, correct, or delete their data. By respecting learners' privacy, we can create a safe and secure learning environment where they can focus on their educational goals without fear of their personal information being misused.

Fairness and equity are essential considerations in ethical design. Educational technology tools should not perpetuate or exacerbate existing inequalities. This means ensuring that tools are accessible to learners from diverse socioeconomic backgrounds, that they do not discriminate based on gender, race, ethnicity, or other personal characteristics, and that they provide equitable opportunities for all learners to succeed. Algorithms used in educational technology should be regularly audited for bias and discrimination, and steps should be taken to mitigate any identified biases.

Inclusivity is another key ethical consideration. Educational technology tools should be designed to as visual and auditory impairments, cognitive differences, and language barriers. By incorporating accessibility features such as screen readers, closed captioning, and alternative text, we can ensure that all learners can participate fully in digital learning experiences.

The potential impact of educational technology on the mental and emotional well-being of learners should also be considered. Tools should be designed to promote positive learning experiences, foster engagement, and avoid causing undue stress or anxiety. This involves incorporating features such as positive feedback mechanisms, adaptive difficulty levels, and opportunities for collaboration and social interaction.

Ethical design also involves considering the long-term consequences of educational technology. As AI and machine learning become more sophisticated, it is important to anticipate the potential impacts of these technologies on learners, educators, and society as a whole. This involves engaging in ongoing dialogue and debate about the ethical implications of AI in education, promoting digital literacy, and advocating for policies that protect individual rights and promote social good in the digital age.

The responsibility for ethical design in educational technology lies with all stakeholders, including developers, educators, policymakers, and learners themselves. Developers should prioritize ethical considerations throughout the design process, from conception to implementation. Educators should be trained on how to evaluate educational technology tools for ethical issues and how to use them in ways that promote positive learning experiences. Policymakers should create regulations and guidelines that encourage ethical design and protect the rights of learners. Learners should be empowered to critically evaluate educational technology tools and advocate for their needs and interests.

By prioritizing ethical considerations in the design of educational technology, we can create tools that empower learners, respect their privacy, promote fairness and equity, and foster positive learning experiences. This requires a collaborative effort from all stakeholders to ensure that educational technology serves the best interests of learners and society as a whole. By embracing ethical design principles, we can harness the power of technology to create a more just, equitable, and inclusive educational landscape for all.

 PPP

"Advocating for ethical policies in digital education is a d responsibility. Staying informed and proactive is essential. Together, we can shape a positive and equitable digital learning environment."

TEN

BUILDING A CULTURE OF RESPECT: FOSTERING AN ONLINE COMMUNITY WHERE RESPECTFUL COMMUNICATION THRIVES.

In the digital landscape, where anonymity and distance can sometimes breed incivility, fostering a culture of respect within online communities is paramount. A respectful online community is one where diverse voices are heard, constructive dialogue flourishes, and individuals feel safe to express themselves without fear of harassment or discrimination. Building such a culture requires intentional effort, clear guidelines, and a collective commitment to civility and empathy.

Respectful communication begins with acknowledging the inherent dignity and worth of every individual. Online interactions should be characterized by courtesy, kindness, and consideration for others' feelings. This means avoiding personal attacks, name-calling, and other forms of verbal abuse. It also means being mindful of the impact of our words and actions on others, even when we disagree with their views.

One of the cornerstones of respectful communication is active listening. This involves paying attention to what others are saying, seeking to understand their perspectives, and responding thoughtfully. It means avoiding interrupting or talking over others, and instead, engaging in a genuine exchange of ideas. Active listening fosters empathy and understanding, which are essential for building bridges across differences and resolving conflicts peacefully.

In addition to active listening, respectful communication involves using inclusive language that avoids stereotypes, generalizations, and discriminatory remarks. It means acknowledging and respecting the diversity of backgrounds, experiences, and perspectives that exist within online communities. By embracing diversity and fostering inclusivity, we create a more welcoming and enriching environment for all.

Clear and consistently enforced community guidelines are essential for fostering a culture of respect. These guidelines should outline acceptable and unacceptable behavior, provide clear examples of respectful and disrespectful communication, and establish consequences for violations. It is important that these guidelines are developed collaboratively, with input from community members, and that they are communicated clearly and consistently.

Moderation plays a crucial role in maintaining a respectful online community. Moderators should be trained to identify and address instances of disrespectful behavior promptly and fairly. This may involve issuing warnings, temporarily suspending users, or, in severe cases, banning them from the community. Moderators should also actively promote positive interactions by highlighting examples of respectful communication and creating opportunities for constructive dialogue.

Technology can also be leveraged to foster a culture of respect online. Many platforms offer features that allow users to report abusive content, block or mute other users, and filter out unwanted comments or messages. These tools can empower individuals to protect themselves from harassment and create a more positive online experience. Additionally, platforms can use algorithms and machine learning to detect and remove harmful content, such as hate speech and misinformation.

Education plays a crucial role in promoting respectful communication online. By teaching digital literacy skills, such as critical thinking, media literacy, and information evaluation, we can empower individuals to navigate the online world responsibly and make informed decisions about their online interactions. It is also important to educate individuals about the potential consequences of their online actions, both for themselves and for others.

Building a culture of respect online is an ongoing process that requires the commitment and participation of all community members. It is not enough to simply avoid disrespectful behavior; we must actively promote positive interactions and create an environment where everyone feels safe, respected, and valued. By embracing diversity, practicing active listening, using inclusive language, and upholding community guidelines, we can create online communities that are not only respectful but also enriching, engaging, and empowering.

The benefits of fostering a culture of respect online extend beyond the virtual realm. Respectful online interactions can spill over into offline relationships, promoting greater understanding and cooperation in the real world. By creating a more positive and inclusive online environment, we can contribute to a more civil and compassionate society as a whole.

ᐅᐅᐅ

"Students must take an active role in promoting ethics in digital learning. Honesty, respect, and critical thinking are their tools. Responsibility in the digital world starts with each individual."

ppp

ELEVEN

Ethical Decision-Making in Action: Practical Strategies for Learners to Make Ethical Choices Online.

In the vast and often uncharted territory of the internet, ethical decision-making is a crucial skill for learners to cultivate. With the abundance of information, diverse communities, and potential for both positive and negative interactions, navigating the online world requires a strong ethical compass. Equipping learners with practical strategies for making ethical choices online empowers them to become responsible digital citizens, fostering a more positive and inclusive online environment for all.

A fundamental principle of ethical decision-making is the Golden Rule: treat others as you would like to be treated. This timeless principle holds true in the digital realm, where the anonymity of the internet can sometimes lead to a disregard for others' feelings and well-being. Before posting a comment, sharing a photo, or engaging in online discussions, consider the impact of your actions on others. Would you want someone to speak to you that way? Would you want your personal information d without your consent? By putting yourself in the shoes of others, you can make more thoughtful and considerate choices online.

Another important strategy is to pause and reflect before acting. In the fast-paced world of the internet, it's easy to react impulsively to a post or comment that triggers an emotional response. However, taking a moment to pause and reflect can help you make a more rational and ethical decision. Ask yourself questions like: What are the potential consequences of my actions? How might my words or actions affect others? Am I contributing to a positive or negative online environment? By taking the time to think before you act, you can avoid making rash decisions that you might later regret.

Critical thinking is an essential skill for ethical decision-making online. With the abundance of information available online, it's important to be able to evaluate the credibility of sources, identify bias, and distinguish between fact and opinion. Don't take everything you read online at face value. Take the time to verify information from multiple sources, consider different perspectives, and question assumptions. By developing your critical thinking skills, you can make more informed and ethical choices about the information you consume and online.

Empathy plays a crucial role in ethical decision-making. Empathy is the ability to understand and the feelings of others. By putting yourself in the shoes of others, you can better appreciate their perspectives and make choices that are considerate of their feelings and well-being. Before posting a comment or engaging in an online discussion, consider how your words might affect others. Are you being respectful and considerate? Are you contributing to a positive or negative online environment? By practicing empathy, you can foster a more compassionate and inclusive online community.

Digital literacy is another essential skill for ethical decision-making online. Digital literacy encompasses a wide range of skills, including the ability to find, evaluate, and use information effectively; to communicate and collaborate online; and to understand the social, ethical, and legal implications of digital technology. By developing your digital literacy skills, you can navigate the online world more safely and responsibly, making informed decisions about your online behavior.

In addition to these individual strategies, there are also collective actions that can be taken to promote ethical decision-making online. Schools and educational institutions can play a crucial role by integrating digital citizenship education into their curricula. This involves teaching students about online safety, privacy, cyberbullying, digital footprints, and the ethical use of technology. Parents can also contribute by having open and honest conversations with their children about their online activities, setting clear expectations for online behavior, and monitoring their children's use of technology.

Online communities can also play a role in promoting ethical decision-making. By establishing clear community guidelines, enforcing those guidelines consistently, and providing resources for resolving conflicts, online communities can create a more positive and respectful environment for all users. Additionally, online platforms can use algorithms and machine learning to detect and remove harmful content, such as hate speech and misinformation.

By employing these practical strategies and working together to create a more ethical online environment, learners can navigate the digital world with confidence and integrity. Ethical decision-making online is not just about avoiding harmful behavior; it's about actively contributing to a positive and inclusive online community where everyone feels safe, respected, and valued. By embracing ethical principles and practicing responsible online behavior, we can harness the power of the internet for good and create a digital world that reflects our highest values.

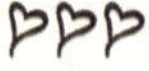

"Collaboration between educators and learners is the foundation of ethical digital learning. Open communication and mutual respect are essential. Together, we build a culture of integrity and responsibility."

❦❦❦

TWELVE

TEACHING DIGITAL CITIZENSHIP: EMPOWERING LEARNERS WITH THE SKILLS AND KNOWLEDGE FOR RESPONSIBLE ONLINE BEHAVIOR.

In an era defined by digital interconnectedness, the concept of digital citizenship has become increasingly vital. It embodies the norms of appropriate, responsible behavior in the online world. Teaching digital citizenship is not merely an addendum to traditional education but a fundamental pillar for preparing learners to navigate the complexities and opportunities of the digital landscape with integrity, empathy, and critical thinking.

Digital citizenship encompasses a broad spectrum of skills and knowledge. It begins with digital literacy, which involves the ability to access, evaluate, and create information using digital technologies. This includes understanding how to navigate online platforms, assess the credibility of sources, and create meaningful digital content. Digital literacy empowers learners to become informed consumers of information and active participants in online communities.

Digital communication is another key component of digital citizenship. This involves understanding the nuances of online communication, including the importance of respectful dialogue, netiquette, and the potential impact of our words on others. Effective digital communication fosters collaboration, builds relationships, and contributes to a positive online environment.

Digital etiquette, or netiquette, is the set of social norms and expectations that govern online behavior. It involves respecting others' opinions, avoiding flaming or trolling, and using appropriate language and tone. Good netiquette promotes civility, creates a welcoming online atmosphere, and encourages constructive dialogue.

Digital safety is a critical aspect of digital citizenship. This involves understanding the risks associated with online activities, such as cyberbullying, phishing scams, and identity theft. It also involves learning how to protect personal information, use strong passwords, and be mindful of one's digital footprint. By prioritizing digital safety, learners can minimize their risk of becoming victims of cybercrime and create a safer online environment for themselves and others.

Digital rights and responsibilities go hand in hand. While

individuals have the right to freedom of expression online, they also have a responsibility to exercise that right responsibly. This means respecting the intellectual property of others, avoiding plagiarism, and refraining from spreading misinformation or hate speech. Digital citizens should also be aware of their rights to privacy and data protection and advocate for policies that uphold these rights.

Digital health and well-being are often overlooked aspects of digital citizenship. Excessive screen time, cyberbullying, and online addiction can have detrimental effects on mental and physical health. It is important for learners to develop healthy habits around technology use, such as taking regular breaks, engaging in offline activities, and seeking help if they experience any negative effects from online interactions.

Digital commerce is another important aspect of digital citizenship. This involves understanding the ethical and legal implications of online transactions, such as online shopping, banking, and investing. It also involves learning how to protect oneself from online scams and fraud. By understanding the principles of digital commerce, learners can make informed decisions about their online financial activities and protect themselves from financial harm.

Teaching digital citizenship requires a multi-faceted approach that involves educators, parents, and the wider community. Schools can integrate digital citizenship education into their curricula, providing students with opportunities to learn about and practice digital citizenship skills in a safe and supportive environment. Parents can play a crucial role by modeling responsible online behavior, discussing online safety and privacy with their children, and setting clear expectations for their children's online activities.

Technology companies also have a responsibility to promote digital citizenship. This involves creating platforms and tools that are safe and user-friendly, providing clear and transparent information about their data collection practices, and taking action against harmful content and behavior.

By empowering learners with the skills and knowledge for responsible online behavior, we can create a more positive and productive digital environment for all. Digital citizenship education is an investment in the future, preparing young people to become active, engaged, and responsible participants in the digital age. As technology continues to evolve and shape our world, the importance of digital citizenship will only grow. By fostering a culture of digital citizenship, we can create a digital landscape that is more equitable, inclusive, and empowering for all.

ᐅᐅᐅ

"Ethics in digital learning is an ongoing journey. As technology evolves, so must our practices. Continuous reflection and adaptation are necessary for a positive educational experience."

❧❧❧

THIRTEEN

THE EDUCATOR'S ROLE: GUIDING ETHICAL DISCUSSIONS AND MODELING ETHICAL BEHAVIOR IN THE DIGITAL CLASSROOM.

In the digital age, the role of educators has expanded beyond traditional instruction to encompass guiding ethical discussions and modeling ethical behavior in the online learning environment. As digital platforms become increasingly integrated into education, educators face the unique challenge of fostering a safe, inclusive, and ethically sound virtual space where students can learn and grow.

Educators play a crucial role in facilitating ethical discussions that help students navigate the complex moral landscape of the digital world. They can introduce students to ethical frameworks and encourage them to critically examine the ethical implications of their online actions. By engaging students in thoughtful discussions about privacy, cyberbullying, plagiarism, and other digital dilemmas, educators can help them develop the critical thinking skills necessary to make informed and responsible choices online.

One effective approach is to create a safe and open space for dialogue where students feel comfortable sharing their thoughts and experiences without fear of judgment. This can involve using case studies, hypothetical scenarios, or real-world examples to spark discussion. Educators can also encourage students to explore different perspectives and consider the potential consequences of their online actions for themselves and others.

In addition to facilitating discussions, educators can model ethical behavior in their own online interactions. This includes demonstrating respect for others' opinions, using inclusive language, avoiding personal attacks, and being mindful of the impact of their words and actions. By embodying ethical principles in their online behavior, educators can set a positive example for their students and create a culture of respect and civility in the digital classroom.

Another important aspect of modeling ethical behavior is promoting digital citizenship. This involves educating students about their rights and responsibilities online, including the importance of protecting their privacy, respecting intellectual property, and engaging in responsible online communication. Educators can incorporate digital citizenship lessons into their curriculum, providing students with the knowledge and skills they need to navigate the online world safely and responsibly.

Educators can also leverage technology to promote ethical behavior in the digital classroom. For instance, they can use online tools to monitor and filter inappropriate content, create private and secure online spaces for discussions, and facilitate collaborative projects that encourage ethical decision-making. By integrating technology into their teaching practices in a thoughtful and intentional way, educators can create a more engaging and enriching learning experience for students while also promoting ethical behavior.

The role of educators in guiding ethical discussions and modeling ethical behavior extends beyond the classroom. They can also collaborate with parents, community leaders, and technology companies to create a more ethical and responsible digital ecosystem. This involves advocating for policies that protect children's privacy online, promoting digital literacy education, and supporting the development of ethical technology tools and platforms.

By working together, educators, parents, and other stakeholders can create a digital environment that is safe, inclusive, and supportive of ethical behavior. This requires ongoing dialogue, collaboration, and a commitment to upholding the highest ethical standards in the digital realm.

The ethical challenges of the digital age are constantly evolving, and educators must be prepared to adapt their teaching practices accordingly. This involves staying up-to-date on the latest technological developments, emerging ethical issues, and best practices for promoting ethical behavior online. By continuously learning and adapting, educators can ensure that they are equipped to guide students through the ever-changing digital landscape in a responsible and ethical way.

In conclusion, educators play a crucial role in guiding ethical discussions and modeling ethical behavior in the digital classroom. By facilitating thoughtful discussions, modeling ethical behavior, promoting digital citizenship, and leveraging technology in a responsible way, educators can empower students to become responsible digital citizens who can navigate the complexities of the online world with integrity, empathy, and critical thinking. By working together with parents, community leaders, and technology companies, educators can also contribute to a more ethical and responsible digital ecosystem that benefits all.

ᐅᐅᐅ

"Educators have the power to shape the future of digital learning. By prioritizing ethics, we can create a better and more equitable educational landscape. Our commitment to integrity and respect will pave the way."

❥❥❥

FOURTEEN

ETHICAL CONSIDERATIONS IN ONLINE ASSESSMENT: CREATING FAIR AND UNBIASED ASSESSMENTS IN THE DIGITAL LEARNING ENVIRONMENT.

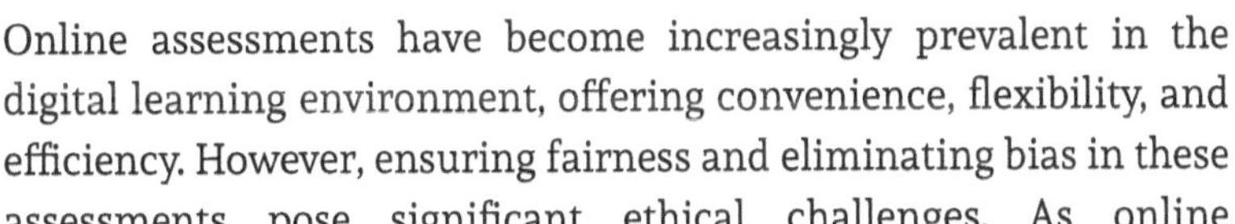

Online assessments have become increasingly prevalent in the digital learning environment, offering convenience, flexibility, and efficiency. However, ensuring fairness and eliminating bias in these assessments pose significant ethical challenges. As online assessments play a crucial role in evaluating student learning and making high-stakes decisions, it is imperative to address these ethical considerations to uphold the principles of equity and justice in education.

One of the primary ethical concerns in online assessment is the potential for unequal access to technology and resources. Not all students have equal access to reliable internet connections, suitable devices, or quiet study spaces. This disparity can create an unfair advantage for those with better resources, while those without may face challenges in completing assessments or demonstrating their full potential. To mitigate this issue, educators need to be mindful of these disparities and offer alternative assessment formats or accommodations for students with limited access to technology.

Another ethical consideration is ensuring the security and integrity of online assessments. The digital environment presents unique challenges in preventing cheating and ensuring that students' work is their own. Online proctoring tools, while helpful in some cases, raise privacy concerns and may not be accessible to all students. Striking a balance between maintaining academic integrity and respecting students' privacy is crucial. Educators can explore alternative methods such as open-book exams, project-based assessments, or collaborative assessments that encourage critical thinking and minimize the temptation to cheat.

The design of online assessments also plays a significant role in ensuring fairness and minimizing bias. Questions should be carefully crafted to avoid cultural references or language that could disadvantage certain groups of students. Additionally, the format and delivery of assessments should be accessible to students with disabilities, ensuring that they have equal opportunities to demonstrate their knowledge and skills. Incorporating universal design principles in online assessments can help create a more inclusive and equitable learning environment.

Algorithmic bias is another ethical concern in online assessments. When algorithms are used to grade or evaluate student work, there is a risk that they may perpetuate or amplify existing biases. If algorithms are trained on biased data, they may produce biased results. It is crucial to scrutinize the algorithms used in online assessments and ensure that they are fair, transparent, and free from discriminatory biases. Regular audits and evaluations of algorithmic systems can help identify and address any potential biases.

The use of data analytics in online assessments raises ethical questions about privacy and surveillance. When student data is collected and analyzed, it is important to be transparent about how the data will be used and to ensure that it is protected from unauthorized access or misuse. Students should be informed about the data collection practices and given the option to opt out if they have concerns. Striking a balance between utilizing data to improve learning experiences and safeguarding student privacy is a delicate ethical challenge that requires careful consideration.

Feedback and transparency are essential components of ethical online assessment. Students should receive timely and constructive feedback on their assessments, highlighting their strengths and areas for improvement. This feedback should be specific, actionable, and focused on learning goals. Transparency in the assessment process, including the criteria for grading and the rationale behind feedback, can help build trust and ensure that students feel they are being assessed fairly.

The ethical considerations in online assessment are not limited to the technical aspects but also extend to the broader context of education. Online assessments should be aligned with the learning objectives of the course and designed to assess the knowledge and skills that are most relevant to students' future success. They should also be used as a tool for learning, not just for evaluation. Formative assessments, which provide feedback during the learning process, can help students identify areas where they need additional support and make adjustments to their learning strategies.

In conclusion, ethical considerations are paramount in creating fair and unbiased assessments in the digital learning environment. Addressing issues such as unequal access to technology, ensuring security and integrity, designing for fairness and inclusivity, mitigating algorithmic bias, protecting privacy, providing feedback and transparency, and aligning assessments with learning goals are all crucial steps in upholding the principles of equity and justice in education. By prioritizing ethical considerations in online assessment, we can create a more equitable and empowering learning environment where all students have the opportunity to succeed.

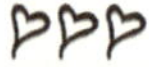

"The digital revolution in education brings incredible opportunities and challenges. Embracing technology with an ethical mindset is crucial. Let us harness its potential while safeguarding our values."

ᗡᗡᗡ

FIFTEEN

Balancing Freedom and Responsibility: Exploring the Ethical Tension Between Online Expression and Responsible Communication.

The digital age has ushered in an era of unprecedented freedom of expression. The internet and social media platforms have given individuals the ability to their thoughts, opinions, and experiences with a global audience. This newfound freedom has empowered marginalized voices, facilitated social movements, and sparked important conversations about pressing social issues. However, the boundless nature of online expression also presents a unique ethical challenge: balancing the right to free speech with the responsibility to communicate responsibly.

Freedom of expression is a fundamental human right enshrined in international law and national constitutions around the world. It is essential for a healthy democracy, fostering a marketplace of ideas where diverse perspectives can be heard and debated. Online platforms have amplified the potential for free expression, allowing individuals to bypass traditional gatekeepers and reach a wider audience than ever before. This has led to a democratization of information and a more inclusive public discourse.

However, the digital landscape is not without its perils. The anonymity and lack of physical proximity afforded by the internet can sometimes embolden individuals to engage in harmful and irresponsible communication. Hate speech, cyberbullying, harassment, and the spread of misinformation are just a few examples of the potential downsides of unfettered online expression. These behaviors can have devastating consequences for individuals and communities, causing emotional distress, social isolation, and even physical harm.

The ethical tension between freedom of expression and responsible communication lies in finding the right balance between these two competing values. While we should protect the right to express diverse opinions, we also have a responsibility to ensure that our words do not cause harm to others. This means being mindful of the potential impact of our online communication, avoiding language that is hateful, discriminatory, or inciting violence, and respecting the dignity and worth of all individuals.

One approach to balancing freedom and responsibility is to

promote digital literacy and critical thinking. This involves teaching individuals how to evaluate the credibility of online sources, identify bias, and distinguish between fact and opinion. By equipping individuals with these skills, we empower them to make informed decisions about the information they consume and online, reducing the spread of misinformation and promoting more responsible communication.

Another approach is to foster a culture of empathy and respect in online communities. This can be achieved through community guidelines, moderation, and educational initiatives that promote civil discourse and discourage harmful behavior. By creating a more positive and inclusive online environment, we can encourage individuals to express themselves freely while also being mindful of the impact of their words on others.

The role of technology companies and social media platforms in balancing freedom and responsibility is also crucial. While these platforms should protect the right to free expression, they also have a responsibility to prevent their platforms from being used to spread hate speech, misinformation, and other harmful content. This may involve implementing content moderation policies, using algorithms to detect and remove harmful content, and partnering with civil society organizations to promote digital literacy and responsible online behavior.

Governments also have a role to play in regulating online expression. While it is important to protect the right to free speech, there are limits to this right. Governments can enact laws that prohibit hate speech, incitement to violence, and other forms of harmful communication. However, it is important to ensure that these laws are narrowly tailored and do not unduly restrict legitimate expression.

The ethical tension between freedom and responsibility is a

complex issue with no easy answers. Striking the right balance requires ongoing dialogue, collaboration, and a willingness to adapt to the changing digital landscape. By promoting digital literacy, fostering a culture of empathy and respect, and implementing responsible content moderation policies, we can create a digital environment that supports free expression while also protecting individuals from harm.

In conclusion, the digital age has ushered in an era of unprecedented freedom of expression, but this freedom comes with the responsibility to communicate responsibly. Balancing these two competing values is a complex ethical challenge that requires a multi-faceted approach. By promoting digital literacy, fostering a culture of empathy and respect, and implementing responsible content moderation policies, we can create a digital environment that supports free expression while also protecting individuals from harm. The ongoing conversation about the ethics of online expression is crucial for ensuring that the digital world remains a space for positive and meaningful dialogue.

"Privacy and security in digital education require vigilance and transparency. Educators must protect student data and foster trust. A respectful and secure learning environment is essential."

❧❧❧

SIXTEEN

THE FUTURE OF ETHICAL LEARNING: ANTICIPATING EMERGING ETHICAL CHALLENGES IN DIGITAL EDUCATION.

The digital landscape is a dynamic and ever-evolving realm, constantly presenting new opportunities and challenges for education. As technology continues to advance at an unprecedented pace, anticipating the emerging ethical challenges in digital education becomes paramount. By proactively addressing these challenges, we can ensure that digital education remains a powerful tool for empowerment and growth, while upholding ethical principles and safeguarding the well-being of learners.

One of the most pressing ethical challenges in the future of digital education is the increasing reliance on artificial intelligence (AI) and machine learning algorithms. While these technologies offer immense potential for personalized learning, adaptive assessments, and intelligent tutoring systems, they also raise concerns about algorithmic bias, data privacy, and the erosion of human agency in the learning process.

Algorithmic bias can manifest in various ways, such as favoring certain demographics over others, perpetuating stereotypes, or limiting access to certain opportunities. As AI becomes more integrated into educational tools and platforms, it is crucial to ensure that these algorithms are transparent, explainable, and free from discriminatory biases. Regular audits and evaluations of algorithmic systems can help identify and address potential biases, ensuring that all learners are treated fairly and equitably.

The collection and analysis of vast amounts of student data by educational technology platforms raise serious privacy concerns. It is imperative to establish robust data protection policies and practices to safeguard sensitive student information from unauthorized access or misuse. Learners should be informed about the data being collected, how it will be used, and who will have access to it. They should also have the right to opt out of data collection or to have their data deleted.

As AI becomes more sophisticated, there is a risk that it may replace human teachers altogether. While AI can automate certain tasks and provide personalized feedback, it cannot replicate the empathy, creativity, and critical thinking skills that human teachers bring to the learning process. The future of ethical digital education lies in finding the right balance between AI and human interaction, leveraging technology to enhance, not replace, the role of teachers.

Another emerging ethical challenge is the potential for virtual and augmented reality (VR/AR) technologies to blur the lines between reality and simulation. While VR/AR can offer immersive and engaging learning experiences, it also raises concerns about the potential for manipulation, addiction, and the erosion of real-world social interaction. It is important to develop ethical guidelines for the use of VR/AR in education, ensuring that these technologies are used responsibly and in ways that promote positive learning outcomes.

The rise of online learning platforms and the increasing availability of open educational resources (OER) have democratized access to education. However, they have also created challenges in ensuring the quality and accreditation of online courses. It is crucial to establish standards for online education that ensure rigor, academic integrity, and the protection of learners' rights. Accreditation bodies need to adapt to the changing landscape of digital education, ensuring that online courses meet the same quality standards as traditional courses.

The globalization of digital education raises ethical questions about cultural sensitivity and inclusivity. As learners from diverse cultural backgrounds interact in online learning environments, it is important to create culturally sensitive content and foster cross-cultural understanding. This involves recognizing and respecting different cultural norms, values, and communication styles. It also means creating inclusive learning environments that are welcoming and supportive of learners from all backgrounds.

The future of ethical learning also involves addressing the digital divide, the gap between those who have access to digital technologies and those who do not. This divide can exacerbate existing educational inequalities and limit opportunities for disadvantaged learners. It is crucial to ensure that all learners have access to affordable and reliable internet, devices, and digital literacy training. This may involve government subsidies, public-private partnerships, or community-based initiatives to expand access to digital resources.

Anticipating and addressing these emerging ethical challenges in digital education requires a collaborative effort from educators, policymakers, technology developers, and learners themselves. By engaging in ongoing dialogue, promoting ethical awareness, and developing robust ethical frameworks, we can ensure that digital education remains a powerful tool for empowerment, equity, and lifelong learning.

ᗞᗞᗞ

"Inclusivity ensures that every student has the opportunity to succeed in the digital world. Access to technology and resources must be universal. Equity in education begins with bridging the digital divide."

ᐅᐅᐅ

SEVENTEEN

CASE STUDIES IN ETHICAL DILEMMAS: REAL-WORLD EXAMPLES OF ETHICAL CHALLENGES FACED BY LEARNERS AND EDUCATORS.

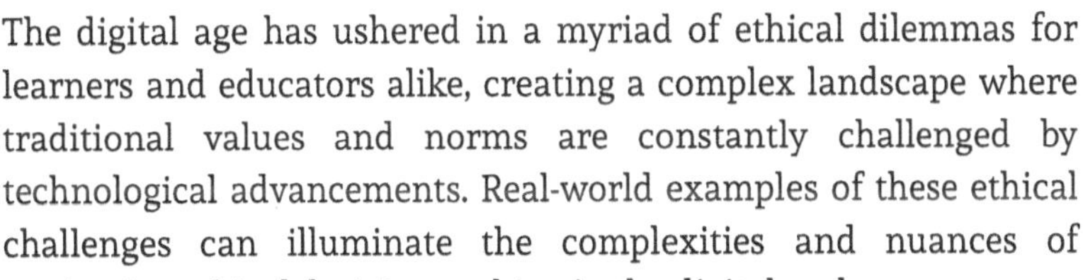

The digital age has ushered in a myriad of ethical dilemmas for learners and educators alike, creating a complex landscape where traditional values and norms are constantly challenged by technological advancements. Real-world examples of these ethical challenges can illuminate the complexities and nuances of navigating ethical decision-making in the digital realm.

Consider the case of a high school student who stumbles upon a classmate's private social media posts revealing personal struggles with mental health. The student is torn between respecting their classmate's privacy and feeling a moral obligation to inform a trusted adult. This dilemma highlights the tension between respecting individual privacy and the duty to protect the well-being of others. In such cases, it is important for educators to provide guidance and create a safe space for students to discuss their concerns and make informed decisions.

The issue of plagiarism in the digital age presents another ethical challenge. A college student, under pressure to submit an assignment, may be tempted to copy and paste information from online sources without proper attribution. While the ease of accessing information online may make plagiarism seem harmless, it is a serious offense that undermines academic integrity and can have long-term consequences for the student's academic and professional career. Educators need to emphasize the importance of original thought, proper citation, and the ethical implications of plagiarism.

The use of artificial intelligence (AI) in education raises ethical questions about the role of technology in the learning process. For instance, AI-powered tutoring systems can provide personalized feedback and support to students, but they also raise concerns about algorithmic bias and the potential for these systems to replace human interaction and connection in the classroom. Educators need to be mindful of these ethical considerations and ensure that AI is used in ways that enhance, not replace, the human element of education.

The proliferation of misinformation and "fake news" online poses a significant challenge for both learners and educators. A student conducting research for a school project may encounter conflicting information from various sources, making it difficult to discern fact from fiction. Educators can help students develop critical thinking skills by teaching them how to evaluate the credibility of online sources, identify bias, and cross-reference information. This can empower students to become discerning consumers of information and active participants in democratic discourse.

Social media platforms present a unique set of ethical challenges, particularly for young learners. The pressure to conform to online norms, the constant comparison to others, and the potential for cyberbullying can have detrimental effects on mental health and well-being. Educators and parents need to equip young people with the skills to navigate social media responsibly, including setting healthy boundaries, managing online interactions, and seeking help if they experience online harassment or bullying.

The use of student data in educational technology also raises ethical concerns. While data analytics can provide valuable insights into student learning patterns and help personalize instruction, it is important to protect student privacy and ensure that data is used ethically and responsibly. This involves obtaining informed consent from students and parents, being transparent about data collection practices, and safeguarding data from unauthorized access or misuse.

The ethical challenges faced by learners and educators in the digital age are complex and multifaceted. There are no easy answers or one-size-fits-all solutions. However, by fostering open dialogue, promoting critical thinking, and establishing clear ethical guidelines, we can create a digital learning environment that is safe, inclusive, and supportive of responsible online behavior.

Educators can play a crucial role in guiding students through these ethical dilemmas, providing them with the tools and knowledge they need to make informed and ethical choices online. By engaging in thoughtful discussions, modeling ethical behavior, and promoting digital citizenship, educators can empower students to navigate the digital world with integrity, empathy, and a sense of social responsibility.

In conclusion, the real-world examples of ethical challenges faced by learners and educators in the digital age highlight the importance of ethical decision-making in the online environment. By addressing these challenges head-on and promoting a culture of ethical awareness and responsibility, we can create a digital landscape that is both empowering and ethically sound. The future of education depends on our ability to navigate the ethical complexities of the digital age and prepare learners to become responsible digital citizens who can use technology for good.

ᐁᐁᐁ

"The ethical use of AI in education demands accountability. Bias must be identified and addressed. Educators have a responsibility to ensure that AI enhances learning without perpetuating inequalities."

❦❦❦

EIGHTEEN

RESOURCES FOR ETHICAL LEARNING: A CURATED LIST OF TOOLS, PLATFORMS, AND ORGANIZATIONS PROMOTING ETHICAL DIGITAL PRACTICES.

Navigating the vast landscape of the digital world can be daunting, especially when it comes to upholding ethical standards and practices. However, a wealth of resources exists to guide and support learners, educators, and institutions in their journey towards ethical digital citizenship. These resources, encompassing tools, platforms, and organizations, offer valuable insights, practical strategies, and educational materials that promote ethical decision-making, responsible online behavior, and the cultivation of a positive digital culture.

For educators seeking to integrate ethical learning into their curriculum, several organizations offer comprehensive resources and frameworks. Common Sense Education provides a wide range of lesson plans, activities, and assessments that cover topics such as digital citizenship, media literacy, and cyberbullying prevention. The International Society for Technology in Education (ISTE) offers standards for students, educators, and leaders that emphasize ethical decision-making, digital citizenship, and responsible use of technology. The Center for Digital Ethics and Policy at Loyola University Chicago offers resources and research on ethical issues related to technology, including privacy, artificial intelligence, and social media.

Numerous online platforms and tools can aid in teaching and promoting ethical digital practices. For instance, Google's Be Internet Awesome program teaches kids the fundamentals of digital citizenship and safety through interactive games and activities. The Cyberwise online hub offers resources for parents, educators, and youth on a variety of topics, including cyberbullying, online privacy, and digital reputation management. The Family Online Safety Institute (FOSI) provides research, education, and advocacy on issues related to online safety and digital citizenship.

For learners of all ages, there are many resources available to help them develop their digital literacy and ethical decision-making skills. The News Literacy Project offers free resources and workshops to help people of all ages learn how to identify credible information and navigate the complex world of online news and information. MediaSmarts provides comprehensive digital and media literacy resources for educators and learners, covering topics such as cyberbullying, privacy, and online hate. Project Zero at Harvard University offers research-based resources and tools for promoting ethical thinking and learning in all subject areas.

In addition to these organizations and platforms, numerous books, articles, and documentaries explore the ethical implications of technology and offer insights into how to navigate the digital world responsibly. The book "Digital Citizenship in Schools" by Mike Ribble and Gerald Bailey provides a comprehensive framework for teaching digital citizenship and responsible technology use. The article "The Ethics of Algorithms" by Cathy O'Neil explores the potential biases and unintended consequences of algorithms used in various aspects of our lives. The documentary "The Social Dilemma" examines the impact of social media on mental health, democracy, and society as a whole.

Libraries play a vital role in promoting ethical digital practices by providing access to information, resources, and technology. They can offer workshops and programs on digital literacy, online safety, and privacy, as well as provide access to online databases and resources on ethical issues related to technology. Librarians can also serve as trusted advisors, guiding learners and educators in their exploration of ethical digital practices.

Social media platforms themselves can be valuable resources for ethical learning. Many platforms have community guidelines and policies that outline acceptable behavior and promote respectful online interactions. They also offer tools for reporting abusive content and blocking or muting other users. By familiarizing themselves with these guidelines and tools, users can contribute to a more positive and inclusive online environment.

The quest for ethical learning in the digital age is an ongoing journey that requires a multi-faceted approach. By utilizing the wealth of resources available, individuals, educators, and institutions can equip themselves with the knowledge, skills, and tools necessary to navigate the digital world ethically and responsibly. By fostering a culture of digital citizenship, critical thinking, and ethical awareness, we can create a digital landscape that is not only technologically advanced but also ethically sound, promoting the well-being of individuals and communities while harnessing the power of technology for good.

ᐅᐅᐅ

"Digital citizenship is a cornerstone of modern education. Respectful and empathetic online behavior must be taught and modeled. Educators play a vital role in guiding students in the digital age."

▷▷▷

NINETEEN

THE ETHICAL LEARNING COMMUNITY

In the digital age, the formation of ethical learning communities is paramount to navigating the complex ethical landscape that technology presents. These communities are not bound by physical walls but rather by a d commitment to ethical digital practices. They are comprised of educators, learners, and stakeholders who collaborate to promote a culture of respect, responsibility, and critical thinking in online spaces. Building such a community is a multifaceted endeavor that requires fostering trust, open communication, and a d sense of purpose.

At the heart of an ethical learning community lies a d understanding of the values and principles that underpin ethical digital practices. This includes a commitment to respect for others, privacy, honesty, integrity, and fairness. Members of the community recognize that their actions online have real-world consequences and that they have a responsibility to use technology in ways that promote positive social outcomes.

Open and transparent communication is crucial for building trust within an ethical learning community. This involves creating spaces where individuals feel safe to express their opinions, ask questions, and challenge assumptions. It also involves being transparent about the use of technology, data collection practices, and decision-making processes.

By fostering open communication, the community can engage in meaningful dialogue about ethical dilemmas, resources and best practices, and collectively address challenges.

Collaboration is another key element of an ethical learning community. Members of the community work together to develop and implement ethical guidelines, policies, and practices. This may involve creating codes of conduct for online behavior, establishing procedures for reporting and addressing unethical behavior, and developing educational resources to promote digital literacy and ethical decision-making.

By collaborating, the community can leverage the collective wisdom and expertise of its members to create a more ethical and responsible digital environment.

Education plays a vital role in building an ethical learning community. This involves providing learners with the knowledge and skills they need to navigate the digital world responsibly. Digital literacy education should not only focus on technical skills but also on critical thinking, media literacy, and ethical decision-making. By equipping learners with these skills, we empower them to become informed and responsible digital citizens who can make ethical choices online.

Educators play a crucial role in modeling ethical behavior and fostering a culture of respect in the digital classroom. They can lead by example, demonstrating responsible online behavior, facilitating respectful dialogue, and addressing instances of unethical behavior promptly and fairly. By creating a safe and supportive learning environment, educators can encourage students to take risks, explore new ideas, and learn from their mistakes.

Parents and caregivers are also important stakeholders in building an ethical learning community. They can partner with educators to reinforce ethical values and practices at home. This may involve discussing online safety and privacy with their children, setting limits on screen time, and monitoring their children's online activities.

By working together, educators and parents can create a consistent message about ethical digital practices and ensure that young people are well-prepared for the challenges and opportunities of the digital age.

The broader community also has a role to play in fostering ethical digital practices. Community leaders, businesses, and policymakers can support the development of ethical learning communities by providing resources, funding, and infrastructure.

They can also advocate for policies that promote digital literacy, protect privacy, and combat cyberbullying and other forms of online harm.

Technology companies also have a responsibility to contribute to building an ethical learning community. This involves designing platforms and tools that are safe, secure, and respectful of users' privacy. It also means being transparent about data collection practices, moderating content to prevent the spread of harmful information, and taking action against unethical behavior on their platforms.

Building an ethical learning community is an ongoing process that requires continuous effort and commitment. It involves adapting to the ever-changing digital landscape, addressing emerging ethical challenges, and fostering a culture of continuous learning and improvement.

By working together, we can create a digital environment that is not only technologically advanced but also ethically sound, promoting the well-being of individuals and communities while harnessing the power of technology for good.

ϷϷϷ

"Content creation and consumption in the digital world require ethical discernment. Misinformation and disrespect have no place in education. Let us empower students to be responsible and thoughtful contributors."

TWENTY

A Call to Action: Inspiring educators and learners to champion ethics in digital learning.

The rapid advancement of technology has revolutionized the landscape of education, bringing about a new era of digital learning. This transformation presents both incredible opportunities and significant challenges, particularly concerning ethics. In a world where information is more accessible than ever, and digital tools offer unprecedented capabilities, the role of educators and learners in championing ethics has become paramount. A call to action is necessary to inspire educators and learners alike to uphold and promote ethical standards in the digital realm, ensuring that the benefits of technological progress are realized while mitigating potential risks and harms.

At the heart of ethical digital learning lies the principle of integrity. Educators must model and instill a commitment to honesty, transparency, and fairness in their students. This begins with the ethical use of digital resources. Plagiarism, once limited to copying from books, has found new avenues in the digital age. The ease with which information can be copied and pasted from the internet poses a significant challenge. Educators must teach students the importance of intellectual property, the value of original thought, and the ethical implications of presenting someone else's work as their own. By emphasizing the importance of proper citation and the creation of original content, educators can foster a culture of integrity that extends beyond the classroom.

Privacy is another critical aspect of ethics in digital learning. The digital age has brought with it an unprecedented level of data collection and surveillance. While these technologies can enhance learning experiences, they also pose significant risks to privacy. Educators must navigate the delicate balance between leveraging data to improve education and protecting the privacy of students. This involves being transparent about the data being collected, its purpose, and how it will be used. It also means advocating for robust data protection policies and teaching students about their digital rights and the importance of safeguarding their personal information. By prioritizing privacy, educators can help build a digital learning environment that respects and protects the individual.

Inclusivity and accessibility are fundamental ethical considerations in digital learning. The digital divide, characterized by disparities in access to technology and the internet, remains a significant barrier to equitable education. Educators must strive to ensure that all students, regardless of their socio-economic status, have access to the tools and resources they need to succeed in a digital learning environment. This includes advocating for policies that provide necessary technology to underserved communities, designing inclusive learning materials that cater to diverse learning needs, and fostering an environment where every student feels valued and supported. By championing inclusivity, educators can help bridge the digital divide and create a more equitable educational landscape.

The ethical use of artificial intelligence (AI) and machine learning in education is another pressing issue. These technologies hold great promise for personalized learning, but they also raise significant ethical concerns. Bias in AI algorithms can perpetuate and even exacerbate existing inequalities. Educators must be vigilant in ensuring that AI tools are used ethically, advocating for transparency in how these tools operate and are trained. They must also educate students about the potential biases in AI and encourage critical thinking about the technology they interact with. By approaching AI with an ethical mindset, educators can help harness its potential while minimizing its risks.

Digital citizenship is a cornerstone of ethical digital learning. It encompasses the responsible use of technology, the importance of respectful online behavior, and the understanding of one's role and rights in the digital world. Educators have a crucial role in teaching students to be good digital citizens. This includes promoting empathy and respect in online interactions, educating students about the potential consequences of cyberbullying, and encouraging the thoughtful and respectful sharing of opinions and information. By fostering a culture of digital citizenship, educators can help students navigate the digital world responsibly and ethically.

The ethical implications of digital content creation and consumption cannot be overlooked. In the age of social media and user-generated content, students are both consumers and creators of digital content. Educators must guide students in understanding the ethical responsibilities that come with content creation, such as the importance of accuracy, the impact of misinformation, and the need for respectful and constructive communication. They must also teach students to critically evaluate the information they encounter online, helping them to discern credible sources from unreliable ones. By promoting ethical content creation and consumption, educators can help students become more discerning and responsible digital citizens.

Another crucial aspect of ethical digital learning is the mental and emotional well-being of students. The digital world can be overwhelming, with constant connectivity leading to issues such as screen fatigue, anxiety, and social isolation. Educators must be mindful of these challenges and take steps to support the well-being of their students. This includes promoting healthy digital habits, such as taking regular breaks from screens, encouraging face-to-face interactions, and fostering a balanced approach to technology use. Educators should also create a supportive environment where students feel comfortable discussing their digital experiences and any associated challenges. By prioritizing well-being, educators can help students navigate the digital world in a healthy and balanced manner.

Ethical digital learning also involves the responsible use of digital tools and resources. Educators must be discerning in their selection of digital tools, ensuring that they align with ethical standards and support the educational goals. This includes evaluating the data privacy policies of digital tools, considering the potential for bias, and ensuring that the tools are accessible and inclusive. By carefully selecting and using digital tools, educators can model ethical behavior and provide students with a positive digital learning experience.

The role of educators in championing ethics in digital learning extends beyond the classroom. They must also advocate for ethical policies at the institutional and governmental levels. This involves staying informed about the latest developments in educational technology and being proactive in addressing emerging ethical issues. Educators can contribute to policy discussions, best practices, and collaborate with other stakeholders to promote ethical standards in digital learning. By taking an active role in shaping the ethical landscape of digital education, educators can help ensure that the benefits of technology are realized while minimizing its risks.

Learners, too, have a vital role in championing ethics in digital learning. They must be proactive in understanding and upholding ethical standards, taking responsibility for their actions in the digital world. This includes being honest in their academic work, respecting the privacy and rights of others, and engaging in respectful and constructive online behavior. Learners should also be critical thinkers, questioning the information they encounter and making informed decisions about the digital tools and resources they use. By taking an active role in promoting ethical digital learning, learners can contribute to a positive and respectful digital learning environment.

Collaboration between educators and learners is essential for fostering an ethical digital learning environment. By working together, they can create a culture of mutual respect, integrity, and responsibility. This involves open communication, where educators and learners can discuss ethical issues, their experiences, and learn from each other. Collaborative projects that focus on ethical digital practices can also be an effective way to reinforce these values. By fostering a collaborative approach, educators and learners can build a strong foundation for ethical digital learning.

The integration of ethics into digital learning is not a one-time effort but an ongoing process. As technology continues to evolve, new ethical challenges will emerge, requiring continuous reflection and adaptation. Educators and learners must remain vigilant, continually assessing and updating their ethical practices to address new developments. This involves staying informed about technological advancements, participating in ongoing professional development, and being open to new ideas and approaches. By committing to ongoing ethical reflection and adaptation, educators and learners can ensure that digital learning remains a positive and enriching experience.

In conclusion, the call to action for inspiring educators and learners to champion ethics in digital learning is a vital and urgent one. The rapid advancement of technology offers incredible opportunities for education, but it also presents significant ethical challenges. By prioritizing integrity, privacy, inclusivity, and well-being, educators and learners can create a digital learning environment that is both enriching and ethical. Through collaboration, critical thinking, and ongoing reflection, they can navigate the complexities of the digital world and harness its potential for positive impact. The responsibility to champion ethics in digital learning lies with all of us, and by rising to this challenge, we can create a better and more equitable educational future.

ԾԾԾ

"The mental and emotional health of students is paramount in the digital era. Encouraging balanced technology use and providing support are essential. Well-being is the foundation of a successful educational journey."

TWENTY-ONE
SUMMARY

The digital revolution has transformed education, bringing new opportunities and challenges. As technology permeates classrooms and learning experiences, integrating ethics into digital learning becomes imperative. "Tech with Heart: Integrating Ethics into Digital Learning" delves into the crucial need to weave ethical considerations into every aspect of digital education, ensuring that the benefits of technology are harnessed while minimizing potential harms. This comprehensive exploration emphasizes the importance of ethical practices in digital learning, covering key areas such as integrity, privacy, inclusivity, the use of artificial intelligence, digital citizenship, content creation and consumption, mental and emotional well-being, responsible use of digital tools, and the roles of educators and learners in fostering an ethical digital learning environment.

At the core of ethical digital learning lies the principle of integrity. The digital age has made it easier than ever to access and information, but it has also increased the risks of plagiarism and intellectual property theft. Educators must model and instill a commitment to honesty and transparency in their students. This involves teaching students the importance of proper citation, the value of original thought, and the ethical implications of presenting someone else's work as their own. By emphasizing the significance of intellectual property and encouraging the creation of original content, educators can cultivate a culture of integrity that extends beyond the digital classroom.

Privacy is another critical component of ethical digital learning. With the proliferation of data collection and surveillance technologies, protecting student privacy has become a significant concern. Educators must navigate the delicate balance between leveraging data to enhance learning experiences and safeguarding the privacy of their students. This involves being transparent about the data being collected, its purpose, and how it will be used. Educators must advocate for robust data protection policies and educate students about their digital rights and the importance of safeguarding their personal information. By prioritizing privacy, educators can help build a digital learning environment that respects and protects the individual.

Inclusivity and accessibility are fundamental ethical considerations in digital learning. The digital divide, characterized by disparities in access to technology and the internet, remains a significant barrier to equitable education. Educators must strive to ensure that all students, regardless of their socio-economic status, have access to the tools and resources they need to succeed in a digital learning environment. This includes advocating for policies that provide necessary technology to underserved communities, designing inclusive learning materials that cater to diverse learning needs, and fostering an environment where every student feels valued and supported. By championing inclusivity, educators can help bridge the digital divide and create a more equitable educational landscape.

The ethical use of artificial intelligence (AI) and machine learning in education is another pressing issue. These technologies hold great promise for personalized learning, but they also raise significant ethical concerns. Bias in AI algorithms can perpetuate and even exacerbate existing inequalities. Educators must be vigilant in ensuring that AI tools are used ethically, advocating for transparency in how these tools operate and are trained. They must also educate students about the potential biases in AI and encourage critical thinking about the technology they interact with. By approaching AI with an ethical mindset, educators can help harness its potential while minimizing its risks.

Digital citizenship is a cornerstone of ethical digital learning. It encompasses the responsible use of technology, the importance of respectful online behavior, and the understanding of one's role and rights in the digital world. Educators have a crucial role in teaching students to be good digital citizens. This includes promoting empathy and respect in online interactions, educating students about the potential consequences of cyberbullying, and encouraging the thoughtful and respectful sharing of opinions and information. By fostering a culture of digital citizenship, educators can help students navigate the digital world responsibly and ethically.

The ethical implications of digital content creation and consumption cannot be overlooked. In the age of social media and user-generated content, students are both consumers and creators of digital content. Educators must guide students in understanding the ethical responsibilities that come with content creation, such as the importance of accuracy, the impact of misinformation, and the need for respectful and constructive communication. They must also teach students to critically evaluate the information they encounter online, helping them to discern credible sources from unreliable ones. By promoting ethical content creation and consumption, educators can help students become more discerning and responsible digital citizens.

Another crucial aspect of ethical digital learning is the mental and emotional well-being of students. The digital world can be overwhelming, with constant connectivity leading to issues such as screen fatigue, anxiety, and social isolation. Educators must be mindful of these challenges and take steps to support the well-being of their students. This includes promoting healthy digital habits, such as taking regular breaks from screens, encouraging face-to-face interactions, and fostering a balanced approach to technology use. Educators should also create a supportive environment where students feel comfortable discussing their digital experiences and any associated challenges. By prioritizing well-being, educators can help students navigate the digital world in a healthy and balanced manner.

Ethical digital learning also involves the responsible use of digital tools and resources. Educators must be discerning in their selection of digital tools, ensuring that they align with ethical standards and support educational goals. This includes evaluating the data privacy policies of digital tools, considering the potential for bias, and ensuring that the tools are accessible and inclusive. By carefully selecting and using digital tools, educators can model ethical behavior and provide students with a positive digital learning experience.

The role of educators in championing ethics in digital learning extends beyond the classroom. They must also advocate for ethical policies at the institutional and governmental levels. This involves staying informed about the latest developments in educational technology and being proactive in addressing emerging ethical issues. Educators can contribute to policy discussions, best practices, and collaborate with other stakeholders to promote ethical standards in digital learning. By taking an active role in shaping the ethical landscape of digital education, educators can help ensure that the benefits of technology are realized while minimizing its risks.

Learners, too, have a vital role in championing ethics in digital learning. They must be proactive in understanding and upholding ethical standards, taking responsibility for their actions in the digital world. This includes being honest in their academic work, respecting the privacy and rights of others, and engaging in respectful and constructive online behavior. Learners should also be critical thinkers, questioning the information they encounter and making informed decisions about the digital tools and resources they use. By taking an active role in promoting ethical digital learning, learners can contribute to a positive and respectful digital learning environment.

Collaboration between educators and learners is essential for fostering an ethical digital learning environment. By working together, they can create a culture of mutual respect, integrity, and responsibility. This involves open communication, where educators and learners can discuss ethical issues, their experiences, and learn from each other. Collaborative projects that focus on ethical digital practices can also be an effective way to reinforce these values. By fostering a collaborative approach, educators and learners can build a strong foundation for ethical digital learning.

The integration of ethics into digital learning is not a one-time effort but an ongoing process. As technology continues to evolve, new ethical challenges will emerge, requiring continuous reflection and adaptation. Educators and learners must remain vigilant, continually assessing and updating their ethical practices to address new developments. This involves staying informed about technological advancements, participating in ongoing professional development, and being open to new ideas and approaches. By committing to ongoing ethical reflection and adaptation, educators and learners can ensure that digital learning remains a positive and enriching experience.

"Tech with Heart: Integrating Ethics into Digital Learning" underscores the urgent need for a concerted effort to embed ethical considerations into every facet of digital education. The rapid advancement of technology offers incredible opportunities for education, but it also presents significant ethical challenges. By prioritizing integrity, privacy, inclusivity, and well-being, educators and learners can create a digital learning environment that is both enriching and ethical. Through collaboration, critical thinking, and ongoing reflection, they can navigate the complexities of the digital world and harness its potential for positive impact. The responsibility to champion ethics in digital learning lies with all of us, and by rising to this challenge, we can create a better and more equitable educational future.

ᐅᐅᐅ

Citation And References

This book represents the culmination of extensive research and meticulous analysis, incorporating a diverse range of sources, including numerous books, scholarly studies, and personal experiences. Additionally, I have scoured various websites to gather relevant information and data essential for the compilation of this work. I have taken every precaution to ensure the accuracy of the information presented and have diligently cited all sources to acknowledge their contributions.

Despite these efforts, the possibility of inadvertent errors remains. I deeply value the insights of my readers and appreciate any feedback that can help identify and rectify such inaccuracies. I encourage you to bring any discrepancies to my attention.

Your feedback is not only welcome but crucial, as it will aid in correcting current editions and enhancing the content of future ones. I am committed to maintaining the highest standards of accuracy and reliability in my work and thank you for your support and understanding.

Additionally, I firmly uphold the principle of freedom of speech and expression as guaranteed under Article 19(1)(a) of the Constitution of India, and I respect the diverse viewpoints and expressions of all readers.

ÞÞÞ

Other Books Of The Author

1. Empowering Minds: A Journey into Women's Self-Discovery and Power
2. The Dynamics of Motivation: Catalyzing Thought into Action
3. Meditation and Mental Well Being: The Path to Inner Peace and Clarity
4. The Psychology of Child Education: Nurturing Future Generations
5. Ethical Enlightenment: A Modern Guide to Living with Integrity
6. Voices of Empowerment: Stories of Women Rising Against Odds
7. Social Psychology in Everyday Life: Understanding Human Connections
8. The Essence of Motivational Speaking: Inspiring Change in Others
9. Balancing Acts: Women, Work, and the Will to Lead
10. Guiding with Grace: Raising Children with Compassion and Awareness
11. The Power of Positive Aging: Embracing Life After Fifty
12. Building Resilient Communities: Social Work in Action
13. The Ethical Educator: Principles for Teaching and Learning
14. From Insight to Impact: Social Psychology for a Better World
15. The Ethics of Empathy: A Guide to Ethical Living
16. The Science of Empowering the Self: Navigating Life's Challenges with Psychological Wisdom
17. The Mindful Conscious Leader: Meditation Techniques for Modern Management
18. Pioneering Spirit: Women's Pathways to Leadership and Empowerment
19. Feeling to Healing: The Role of Emotional Intelligence in Child Development
20. Transformative Talks and Words of Inspiration: Insights into Motivational Oratory

21. Green Ethics: A Path to Sustainable Living
22. Spiritual Integrity: Navigating Life with Moral Compassion
23. Clean Living, Clean Society: The Ethics of Cleanliness
24. Patriotic Spirits: Building a Nation on Positive Attitudes
25. Innovative Integrity & Vibrant Visions: The Ethical and Entrepreneurial Spirit of Gujarat
26. Youthful Visions, Endless Possibilities: Inspiring Ethics and Motivation in Children
27. Living Your Legacy: How to Motivate Others by Living Your Values
28. Secret of Healing Conversations: Ethical Practices in Counselling and Therapy
29. Creative Kindness: Crafting a Life of Compassion and Creativity
30. The Power of Appreciation: How Gratitude Can Transform Your Relationships
31. Bhagavad-Gita: Messages
32. Science of Art: The New Frontier of Fashion Modernism
33. Vivekananda's Virtues: A Blueprint for Modern Living
34. Empower Her: Navigating the Path to Women's Entrepreneurship
35. The Boundless Classroom: Innovations in Global Education
36. The Language of Leadership: Communicating with Authenticity and Impact
37. The Warrior's Mantra: Deciphering the Hanuman Chalisa
38. Echoes of Empathy: Transformative Stories of Social Service
39. Artful Living: Cultivating Creativity in Your Daily Routine
40. Finding Your Why: Discovering Your Passions and Charting Your Course
41. The Role of Social Media in Shaping Self-Esteem and Interpersonal Relationships among Adolescents
42. Karma's Tapestry: Weaving a Life of Selfless Service
43. Altruistic Alchemy: Transforming Lives Through Giving
44. The Blueprint of Pro-Activeness and Productivity: Crafting Habits for Success
45. The Simplicity with Grounded Wisdom: Embracing Authenticity

in a Complex World

46. Secret of Solopreneur's Odyssey: Navigating the Path to Self-Employment
47. Exploring Tapestry of Peace: Global Perspectives on Harmony
48. The Art and Actions of Connection: Mastering Communication for Impact
49. She Governs and at the Helm: Strategies for Political Empowerment
50. Rising Above and Rising with Grace: A Woman's Roadmap to Career Mastery
51. The Effect of Networking & Connectedness: Building Strategic Alliances for Women
52. Beyond his Barriers: Women Thriving in Male-Dominated Fields
53. Secret of Inner Compass: Navigating Life with Intuition
54. Creative & Pro-Active Muses: A Celebration of Women in the Arts
55. Unburdened: The Art of Releasing the Past
56. Amplified Voices: Speeches of Women that Astonished the World
57. Secret of Manifesting Dreams: A Woman's Guide to Intentional Living
58. Ethics and Value Based Education: Reimagining Japan's School System
59. The Moral Compass Curriculum: A Holistic Approach
60. Tech with Heart: Integrating Ethics into Digital Learning
61. Honoring Virtue: Recognizing Ethical Excellence in Education
62. Raising Good Humans: A Guide to Character Development
63. The Spark Within: Nurturing Creativity in Children
64. The Teenager Whisperer: Navigating Adolescence with Grace
65. Igniting a Passion for Learning: Inspiring Lifelong Curiosity
66. The Habit Lab: Cultivating Positive Behaviors in Children
67. Seeds of Empathy: Fostering Compassion in Young Hearts
68. The Reading Revolution: Inspiring a Love of Books in Children
69. The Learning Brain: Unlocking the Secrets of Student Success
70. Teaching for All: Differentiated Instruction Strategies
71. The Time Alchemist: Mastering Time Management for Peak Performance

Bhajan
101.   Pilgrimage of the Soul: Spiritual Journeys in India

ᐅᐅᐅ

Contact

Dr. Minakshi Bansal
Social Activist
Ahmedabad, Gujarat, Bharat
minakshiindiag20@yahoo.com

❦❦❦

|| LOKAHA SAMASTHAHA SUKHINO BHAVANTU ||

www.ingramcontent.com/pod-product-compliance
Lightning Source LLC
Chambersburg PA
CBHW020542160726
47991CB00002B/552